1. Introduction

The Great Recession, as has been widely noted, differs from other post-WWII downturns in terms of severity and persistence; we explore whether it also differs in terms of its impact on productivity-enhancing reallocation. A pervasive feature of the U.S. economy is a high pace of output and input reallocation across producers.[1] The annual average job creation rate for the U.S. private sector over the last 30 years is close to 18 percent while the analogous job destruction rate is 16 percent. Evidence shows this high pace of reallocation is closely linked to productivity dynamics. That is, resources are shifted away from low productivity producers towards high productivity producers. An open question is whether recessions are "cleansing," in that they are periods in which this productivity-enhancing reallocation is accelerated. Theory suggests the nature and extent of productivity-enhancing reallocation could be fundamentally altered by the nature of the downturn. Using micro-level data, we examine how the pattern of reallocation differs in the Great Recession in terms of both intensity and the extent to which it was productivity-enhancing.

The cleansing hypothesis is that the opportunity cost of time and resources are low during recessions implying recessions are times of accelerated productivity enhancing reallocation.[2] Prior research suggests the recession in the early 1980s is consistent with an accelerated pace of productivity enhancing reallocation.[3] Alternative hypotheses that work against cleansing effects highlight the potential distortions to reallocation dynamics in recessions. Such distortions could arise from many factors including, for example, distortions to credit markets. When credit markets are distorted in recessions, reallocation may be driven more by credit constraints and less by market fundamentals such as productivity, demand and costs. The close connection between the financial crisis and the Great Recession suggests this hypothesis might be especially relevant in the recent period.

---

[1] We use productivity differences across producers as a placeholder more generally for differences across producers in terms of technical efficiency, demand and costs. All of these factors contribute to our empirical measure of establishment-level productivity as we discuss below.

[2] It is important to emphasize the finding that reallocations are "cleansing" is not a statement that recessions are welfare enhancing. The social planner may prefer to avoid cyclical variation in activity along with the loss of activity from unemployment. But, conditional on the cycle occurring, the social planner may have found it optimal to increase the pace of productivity-enhancing reallocation given the opportunity cost of time is low.

[3] Foster, Haltiwanger and Krizan (2001) find the 1977-82 and 1982-87 periods were times of especially intense productivity enhancing reallocation. Davis, Haltiwanger and Schuh (1996) highlight the increased intensity of reallocation during the 1982-83 recession. They find this was especially apparent in the U.S. steel industry, which exhibited an accelerated intense reallocation away from integrated mills and towards mini-mills during the early 1980s. Recent research by Collard-Wexler and De Loecker (2013) shows this type of reallocation was responsible for much of the productivity growth in the U.S. steel industry over the last several decades.

Our empirical analysis begins with analyzing patterns of job reallocation over the business cycle for the entire U.S. economy. For this part of the analysis, we rely primarily on data from the Business Dynamics Statistics (BDS) series, which provides annual job flow statistics for the entire U.S. private sector. We supplement this with analysis of quarterly job flow statistics from the Business Employment Dynamics (BED) statistics, which also cover the U.S. private sector. We compare patterns in job creation and destruction in the Great Recession to the post-1980 recessions. Our analysis of reallocation dynamics over the cycle exploits not only the national business cycle but also state business cycles. An obvious challenge for macroeconomic empirical work is the relatively short time series and limited number of cyclical episodes inherent in such analysis. These challenges are exacerbated in our analysis since we use annual BDS job creation and destruction measures for 1981 through 2011.[4] We overcome the inherent degrees of freedom limitations by using job flow measures at the state-by-year level of aggregation. In a similar fashion, we exploit state cycles in our later establishment-level analysis of the cyclicality of the connection between productivity and reallocation.

We find there is a notable change in the responsiveness of job creation and destruction to cyclical contractions in the Great Recession relative to the responsiveness in prior recessions. We find that in prior recessions, periods of economic contraction exhibit a sharp increase in job destruction and mild decrease in job creation. As highlighted by Davis and Haltiwanger (1990, 1992, 1999), the greater responsiveness of job destruction relative to job creation in these earlier cyclical downturns implies recessions are times of increased reallocation. However, in the Great Recession, job creation fell by as much or more than the increase in job destruction. In this respect, the Great Recession was not a time of increased reallocation (whether productivity enhancing or not).

The second part of our analysis investigates the relationship between productivity and reallocation - how it varies over the cycle in general and the extent to which it changed in the Great Recession in particular. Earlier research shows a tight connection between reallocation and productivity dynamics. That is, exit is much more likely for low productivity establishments while establishment growth is increasing in productivity. Earlier research has also found a large fraction of industry-level productivity growth is accounted for by this reallocation of outputs and

---

[4] We commence our analysis in 1981 to make it possible to classify establishments into two age classes - those belonging to firms less than five years old and five plus years old. The LBD has left-censored firm age for firms that started in 1976 or before.

inputs from low productivity to high productivity businesses.[5] This connection between reallocation and productivity dynamics has been shown to be driven in part by selection and learning dynamics of young establishments (typically part of young firms). In any given year there is a wave of establishment (and firm) entry. Most new establishments do not survive, but among those that do survive are fast growing, high productivity establishments. The young (and mature) establishments that do not survive have much lower productivity than more mature, incumbent establishments (in the same industry).

While we are able to characterize job reallocation dynamics for the entire U.S. private sector, our analysis of the relationship between reallocation and productivity dynamics over the cycle is restricted to the U.S. manufacturing sector. In order to measure productivity at the establishment level, we rely on data from the Census of Manufactures (CM) and the Annual Survey of Manufactures (ASM). We find job creation and destruction dynamics for manufacturing largely mimic the patterns for the whole economy. In prior recessions, job destruction increases more than job creation falls in the manufacturing sector. However, in the Great Recession, there is a larger response of job creation than in prior recessions. We find some differences between the overall private and manufacturing sectors in terms of their cyclical dynamics of job flows in the Great Recession. Despite these differences, we believe our micro-based analysis of the connection between productivity and establishment-level survival and growth should be of relevance more broadly as well.

Consistent with the existing literature, we find evidence that reallocation is productivity enhancing in the manufacturing sector. We find establishment exit is substantially more likely for low productivity establishments compared to high productivity establishments. In addition, we find growth is a strongly increasing function of establishment-level productivity for continuing establishments.

Turning to how these patterns vary over the business cycle, it is useful to note we find exit increases and growth of continuing establishments declines during cyclical contractions. We also find the cyclical responsiveness of exit and growth to contractions is especially large in the Great Recession.

For the main questions of interest, we find the marginal impact of productivity on exit and growth changes over the cycle. For recessions before the Great Recession, the marginal impact of productivity on growth increases with the magnitude of the contraction. However, in

---
[5] See for example, Baily, Hulten, and Campbell (1992) and Foster, Haltiwanger and Krizan (2001, 2006).

the Great Recession, the marginal impact of productivity on growth decreases with the magnitude of the contraction. It is still the case that more productive establishments have higher growth rates in the Great Recession (at least for the range of cyclical changes we observe) but the difference in the growth rate between high and low productivity establishments declines with sharp contractions. We decompose the overall effect of productivity on growth into the exit margin and the impact on the growth of continuing establishments. We find patterns for overall growth are driven especially by the exit margin. We also find these effects are larger for establishments of young firms – suggesting changing patterns in the relationship between productivity, growth and survival are primarily driven by young firms.[6]

The paper proceeds as follows. The next section provides a literature review. Section 3 describes the data and measurement issues. In Section 4, we analyze job reallocation over the business cycle. We bring together reallocation and productivity measures in Section 5 to address our central research question about the cleansing effect of the Great Recession. Section 6 concludes and offers ideas for future related areas of research.

2. Literature Review

Whether recessions are a period of productive winnowing or counterproductive destruction has been the subject of a long ongoing debate. Economists trace the genesis of the debate back to the Schumpeter's (1939, 1942) discussion of creative destruction. Using micro-level datasets which enable direct empirical analysis of the cleansing impact of recessions, Davis and Haltiwanger (1990, 1992, 1999) show job reallocation activity increased during recessions in the manufacturing sector. Extending the analysis to the entire private sector, Davis, Faberman and Haltiwanger (2006, 2012) find these patterns for manufacturing also hold for the entire private sector.

Davis and Haltiwanger (1990, 1992, 1999) highlight a simple property of the relationship between the relative cyclicality of job creation and destruction and overall job reallocation. The latter is measured in this literature as the sum of job creation and destruction. It follows directly that if job creation and job destruction move in equal and opposite directions during a cyclical downturn, then job reallocation does not change. If job destruction rises more than job creation

---

[6] Fort et al. (2013) find young and small firms are hit especially hard in the Great Recession. They find the decline in housing prices is important in that context.

falls, then reallocation increases while if the opposite holds then job reallocation falls.[7]

Davis and Haltiwanger (1990, 1992) relate these possible empirical patterns to models of reallocation timing. They note in models where the marginal cost of creating jobs is lower in recessions, reallocation should increase in recessions implying job destruction should be more responsive than job creation to cyclical shocks.[8] This property is also present in Caballero and Hammour's papers on the cleansing effect of recessions. Caballero and Hammour (1994) develop a model illustrating the conditions under which reallocation will be both more intense in recessions and cleansing in the sense that more intense reallocation will be associated with moving resources from less productive to more productive producers.

In their 1996 paper, Caballero and Hammour highlight potential distortions in cyclical reallocation dynamics. In particular, they note if the marginal cost of creating jobs is lower in recessions, then the social planner would have job creation and destruction rise in recessions (with destruction leading job creation but only to the extent that there are search, matching and other frictions the social planner cannot overcome). They in turn emphasize recessions with strong decoupling of job creation and destruction (a rise in job destruction, a decline in job creation and only a very slow recovery in job creation) are a sign of inefficiency. The distortions Caballero and Hammour emphasize are hold up problems and bargaining problems that may distort the incentives for job creation and job destruction.

Beyond the distortions emphasized by Caballero and Hammour (1996), there are numerous mechanisms that can yield sullying or scarring effects of recessions. Barlevy (2003) develops a model that builds on the credit market imperfections of Bernanke and Gertler (1989). In his model, recessions tend to be cleansing in the absence of financial constraints. However, when financial constraints are present, a countervailing force has the potential to reverse the cleansing effect of recessions. The best projects are those that require the most funding so credit market constraints actually hit hardest for projects with greater surplus since these are also the projects with the highest start-up costs. When there are financial constraints, recessions are times when the best jobs will be destroyed. An aggregate shock affecting profitability (such as a

---

[7] Blanchard and Diamond (1990), Davis and Haltiwanger (1990,1999) and Caballero and Hammour (2005) use VAR analysis to conduct a more nuanced and sophisticated analysis of the behavior of job reallocation over the cycle. As they emphasize, exploring the cumulative impulse response functions of job creation, destruction and - in turn - reallocation in response to an econometric specification that explicitly identifies the aggregate shocks provides a more comprehensive analysis than simple descriptive statistics of the cyclical patterns of job creation, destruction and reallocation. Given we do not conduct such analysis here, our characterization of the cyclical dynamics of creation and destruction here should be viewed as suggestive.

[8] They develop such a reallocation model but note that the Mortensen and Pissarides (1994) framework has this property.

negative productivity shock), "tightens the incentive constraints on entrepreneurs leading to a shift of resources towards projects that require less credit and yield less surplus. Thus, recessions will be associated with increased reallocation, but this reallocation will no longer serve to foster a more efficient mode of production (p. 1800)." There are two predictions here: recessions are times of increased reallocation and the reallocation is not cleansing.[9]

Using a model calibrated with the Business Employment Dynamics data, Osotimehin and Pappadà (2013), show that while credit frictions (consistent with those described by Bernanke and Gertler, 1989) have a distortionary effect on the selection of exiting firms, they do not reverse the cleansing effect of recessions. The contrast between their conclusion and that of Barlevy (2003) rests on assumptions about characteristics of firms that differ by productivity. While Barlevy argues the most productive businesses are likely to be more subject to credit constraints, Osotimehin and Pappadà believe the most productive firms face more forgiving net-worth exit thresholds and are more likely to face better draws of idiosyncratic productivity shocks (due to the persistence of productivity).[10]

Most of these models have as antecedents (or can be related to) the canonical models of firm dynamics by Jovanovic (1982), Hopenhayn (1992), Hopenhayn and Rogerson (1993) and Ericson and Pakes (1995). These classic models provide a structure for heterogeneous firm dynamics models where firms are subject to idiosyncratic productivity, demand and cost shocks, which impact their growth and survival. Moreover, these models highlight that entering businesses face uncertainty about their prospects. This implies selection and learning dynamics are a critical feature of firm dynamics, especially for young firms. The theoretical and empirical literature on productivity and reallocation is based on these canonical models. As such, the literature on how patterns of productivity and reallocation vary over the cycle builds on these foundations.

Empirical work on the connection between reallocation and productivity has mostly focused on low frequency variation (e.g., variation over 5 years or over a decade).[11] A few

---

[9] Barlevy has another relevant paper focusing on a different possible reason for sullying effects in recessions. Barlevy (2002) focuses on the hypothesis that bad worker matches are less likely to be terminated in recessions given the decline in quits in recessions. These sullying effects are more about churning or excess worker flows than job flows. That is, his hypotheses are more about whether workers are well matched rather than whether production sites are well suited for production. Given our focus on job flows, we are more concerned about the latter.
[10] Other mechanisms that work against cleansing have been proposed. For example, Ouyang (2009) argues recessions stifle opportunities for learning that are important for the development of young firms.
[11] See, for example, the survey papers by Syverson (2011) and Bartelsman and Doms (2000).

papers have explored how the patterns vary over the cycle.[12] Foster, Haltiwanger and Krizan (2001) use micro-level data to decompose aggregate (industry level) productivity growth into within-establishment productivity growth and productivity growth resulting from the reallocation of activity from less productive to more productive establishments.[13] They find a large fraction of U.S. manufacturing productivity growth is accounted for by shifting activity from less productive to more productive establishments. While their focus is not the cycle, they look at cyclical patterns by examining three 5-year periods (1977-82, 1982-87 and 1987-92). They find the contribution of both between-establishment reallocation and net entry to productivity growth are especially large during the 1977-82 period, which corresponds roughly to a cyclical downturn.[14]

Using Colombian establishment-level data, Eslava et al. (2010) present empirical evidence that the exit margin is distorted in times of financial constraints in a manner consistent with the model of Barlevy (2003). High productivity firms exit during recessions because they are credit constrained, while other less productive, not credit-constrained firms survive. An establishment in the lowest 10th TFP percentile without credit constraints has the same exit probability as an establishment in the 39th TFP percentile with credit constraints.

We now turn to our own empirical analyses of similar questions. We address four questions concerning the potential cleansing effects of the Great Recession. First, do patterns of reallocation over the business cycle change in the Great Recession? Second, is reallocation productivity enhancing? Third, does the nature of the relationship between productivity and reallocation change over the business cycle? Fourth, is the relationship between productivity and reallocation we see in earlier recessions different in the Great Recession? While we do not

---

[12] Lee and Mukoyama (2012) use establishment-level data to look at reallocation and productivity over the business cycle. They find exit rates and the productivity of exiters do not vary much over the cycle while entry rates and the productivity of entrants vary substantially over the cycle. It is difficult to compare their results to ours given they faced key data limitations (they did not have access to the LBD so they had to exclude all first years of ASM panels) and they used only national variation in the cycle (so their conclusions are based on a small number of observations in terms of the cycle). We also think their results are sensitive to their non-standard timing of recessions and booms given the nature of the ASM data they use. For example, they classify 1983 as a "good" (i.e., expansion) year in their analysis. The job flow statistics they use from Davis, Haltiwanger and Schuh (DHS, 1996) are based on March-to-March changes so 1983 statistics reflect March 1982 to March 1983. The DHS statistics show that over this period the manufacturing sector had a sharp net contraction in employment (one of the three largest over the entire sample). Campbell (1998) uses entry and exit statistics from DHS (1996) to examine whether shocks to technological shocks are a significant driver of business cycles. He finds entry rates are procyclical and vary positively with productivity growth, while exit rates are countercyclical and do not vary with contemporaneous productivity growth.
[13] They use accounting decompositions related to those developed by Baily, Hulten and Campbell (1992), Griliches and Regev (1995) and Olley and Pakes (1996).
[14] Baily, Bartelsman and Haltiwanger (2001) examine labor productivity over the cycle and find evidence reallocation during recessions is productivity enhancing.

directly address any potential reasons for differences, we are interested in whether the patterns we find are suggestive of underlying causes. The next section describes our data and related measurement issues.

3. Data and Measurement Issues

We describe our measures of reallocation and productivity in this section. We rely heavily on the growing existing literature on measuring these concepts using micro-level data. Our primary data sources are administrative, census and survey establishment-level data from the U.S. Census Bureau. These annual data cover the period from about the mid-1970s to 2011, thus enabling us to compare the Great Recession to earlier recessions.[15] We are able to examine reallocation for the entire U.S. economy, but for reasons of data availability, are constrained to the manufacturing sector when analyzing productivity. We begin by describing how we measure reallocation over the business cycle (this relates to the analysis in Section 4). We then describe how we measure productivity and reallocation in an integrated manner (this relates to the analysis in Section 5).

3.1 Reallocation

Our annual job reallocation measures for the entire U.S. economy and the manufacturing sector are from the public-use Business Dynamics Statistics (BDS) series. The BDS is a public-use dataset derived from the Longitudinal Business Database (LBD).[16] The LBD is a longitudinally linked version of the Census Bureau's business register. As such, the LBD covers all establishments with paid employees in the non-agricultural private sectors of the U.S. economy (see Jarmin and Miranda, 2002).

Measures of job flows in the BDS are consistent with the methodology from Davis, Haltiwanger and Schuh (1996) (henceforth DHS). DHS measure job creation as the employment gains from all expanding establishments including startups and job destruction as the employment losses from all contracting establishments including shutdowns. These measures are built up from establishment-level growth rates. Let E_{it} be employment at establishment i in year t; i.e., the number of workers on the payroll in the pay period covering March 12. The

---

[15] We use a variety of data sources some of which cover different periods. The public domain BDS has job flows from 1977 to 2011. The internal version of the LBD, on which the BDS is based, is available from 1976 to 2011. The ASM/CM data we use to measure productivity is available from 1972 to 2010. We integrate this with the LBD so we can examine outcomes in the LBD from t to $t+1$ (starting in 1981 and looking at outcomes through 2011) using productivity through 2010.

[16] BDS data are available at http://www.census.gov/ces/dataproducts/bds/.

employment growth rate is $g_{it} = (E_{it} - E_{it-1})/X_{it}$, where $X_{it} = .5*(E_{it} + E_{it-1})$.[17] The employment growth rate at any higher level of aggregation is the weighted mean of establishment growth rates given by $g_t = \sum_i (X_{it}/X_t)g_{it}$, where $X_t = \sum_i X_{it}$. The job creation rate is the employment-weighted average of the growing establishments including startups, and the job destruction rate is the employment-weighted average of the shrinking establishments including shutdowns. The job reallocation rate is the sum of the job creation and job destruction rate. More detail on these measures is provided in the Appendix.

Measures of reallocation can be calculated for various groups of establishments including establishment age and firm age groups, establishment and firm size groups, establishment location (region, state) groups and establishment industry groups.[18] In addition, the measures of reallocation can be disaggregated into intensive and extensive margins. Establishment births are those establishments that did not exist in time t-1, but exist in time t; analogously establishment deaths are those establishments that exist in time t-1, but do not exist in time t. All designations of births and deaths rely upon the complete universe of information from the LBD.[19]

While most of our analysis of job flows relies on the BDS, we supplement this analysis with an alternative public domain source of jobs flows. The Business Employment Dynamics (BED) is a longitudinal version of Bureau of Labor Statistics' (BLS) Quarterly Census of Employment and Wages. The BED covers the private economy and thus provides a quarterly analog to the annual data provided by the BDS (although coverage and measurement issues make comparability complicated).[20] The methodology for measuring job flows in the BED is essentially the same as that for the BDS.[21]

---

[17] This growth rate measure has become standard in analyses of establishment and firm dynamics because it shares some useful properties of log differences while also accommodating entry and exit. See DHS (1996) and Tornqvist, Vartia and Vartia (1985) for discussion.

[18] We follow Haltiwanger, Jarmin and Miranda (2013) in our measurement and definitions of establishment and firm size and age. Age of a firm is based on the age of the oldest establishment at the time of the new firm's inception. After that, a firm ages naturally regardless of changes in composition. See Haltiwanger, Jarmin and Miranda (2013) for more on the distinction between establishments and firms in the LBD.

[19] The establishment links in the LBD are of high quality given the comprehensive administrative data underlying the LBD. DHS(1996) rely upon the ASM and CM to create measures of job creation and destruction using Census micro-level data. Using the ASM, with its rotating panels of establishments, introduces measurement complexities we avoid by using the LBD. See the Appendix for further discussion.

[20] See Davis, Faberman and Haltiwanger (2012) for a discussion of the cyclical dynamics of job flows in the BED. See Haltiwanger, Jarmin and Miranda (2011) for a discussion of the cyclical dynamics of job flows in the BDS.

[21] We use BED statistics from Davis, Faberman and Haltiwanger (2012) that have been extended back to 1990:2.

3.2 Connection Between Productivity and Reallocation

To explore the connection between productivity and reallocation, we use establishment-level data from the U.S. Census Bureau. We integrate the establishment-level LBD with establishment-level data from the Annual Survey of Manufactures (ASM) and the Census of Manufactures (CM). We provide an overview of our data and construction of measures in this section, and provide more detail in the Appendix.

We begin by identifying all manufacturing establishments in the LBD from 1976 to 2011. We compute measures of growth and survival using the DHS methodology discussed above for these establishments. Specifically, we generate measures of DHS growth rates at the establishment-level, which can accommodate establishment-level entry and exit. In turn, we generate indicators of the components of growth –DHS growth rates for continuing establishments and indicators of establishment entry and exit. All of these measures are based on the full LBD and do not require any information from the ASM/CM data. Our measures of firm size and firm age are also derived from the full LBD and are not dependent on the ASM/CM data. In developing these growth rate and outcome measures, we adopt the timing convention that the growth rate from March of year t to March of year $t+1$ represents the t to $t+1$ growth rate (e.g., a 2010 outcome reflects the change from March 2010 to March 2011). Thus, our analysis of the connection between productivity and reallocation reflects outcomes from t to $t+1$ as a function of establishment-level TFP and other measures (e.g., firm size and firm age) in period t. We now turn to how we construct establishment-level measures of TFP in year t.

To construct a measure of TFP to integrate with these LBD measures, we rely on the sub-sample of establishments present each year in either the ASM or CM from 1972-2010. While we use data back to 1972 to get the best possible capital stock measures, our analysis uses data from 1981-2010. We focus on this period since we are interested in classifying establishments based on the age of their parent firm. Our firm age measure is left-censored for firms born in or before 1976. As such in 1981 and beyond, we can consistently classify firms into age classes of less than 5 and 5 or more years old.

First, we briefly discuss the nature of the sub-sample. The CM is, in principle, the universe of establishments, but data are collected only from those establishments mailed forms. Very small establishments (where the size threshold varies by industry) have their data imputed from administrative data. We exclude those cases. The CM is collected every 5 years in years ending in "2" and "7". The ASM is collected in all years where a CM is not collected and is a sample of roughly 50,000-70,000 manufacturing establishments. Probability of selection in to the ASM sample is a function of industry and size. Thus, in both ASM and CM years, we have a subset of establishments of the comprehensive universe from the LBD. To deal with this issue, we estimate propensity score weights for each establishment-year observation in the LBD. The weights are based on the probability an establishment is in the ASM or CM (non administrative record cases) in a specific year. As we show in the Appendix, using such propensity score weights enables our weighted sample to replicate the size, age and industry distributions in the LBD as well as the overall patterns of employment in the LBD. Note we estimate the propensity score models separately for each year which enables us to take into account the changing nature of our samples (e.g., CM vs. ASM years). For all of our statistical analysis using the matched ASM/CM/LBD data, we use these propensity score weights.[22]

We now turn to how we measure TFP at the establishment level. We construct an index in a manner similar to that used in Baily, Hulten and Campbell (1992) and a series of papers that built on that work.[23] The index is given by:

$$lnTFP_{et} = lnQ_{et} - \alpha_K lnK_{et} - \alpha_L lnL_{et} - \alpha_M lnM_{et} \qquad (1)$$

where Q is real output, K is real capital, L is labor input, M is materials, α denotes factor elasticities, the subscript e denotes individual establishments and the subscript t denotes time. Details on measurement of output and inputs are in the Appendix, so here we focus on the most relevant features of how these various components are measured. Operationally, we define nominal output as total shipments plus the change in inventories. Output is deflated using an industry-level measure from the NBER-CES Manufacturing Industry Database. Capital is measured separately for structures and equipment using a perpetual inventory method. Labor is measured as total hours of production and non-production workers. Materials are measured separately for physical materials and energy and where each are deflated by an industry level deflator. Outputs and inputs are measured in constant 1997 dollars.

We measure the factor elasticities using industry-level cost shares (of total factor costs). Operationally, we could measure these factor elasticities at the establishment level. However, arguments against using an establishment-level approach can be made when factor adjustment

---

[22] The ASM has sample weights, which could in principle be used instead. However, the sample weighted ASM is not designed to match published totals as discussed in DHS (1996). Moreover, our method implies we are capturing the patterns of the universe LBD data. Finally, our method facilitates using the CM and ASM records in a consistent manner.

[23] Syverson (2011) provides an excellent summary.

costs exist (see Syverson, 2011). Moreover, for related reasons, Syverson (2011) notes some time averaging may be warranted at the industry-level. Accordingly, for an establishment in a given industry in period t, we use industry-level measures of cost shares for period t based on the average of the t and t-1 cost share for the factor elasticity.[24]

Given the large differences in output measures across industries (for example, steel versus food), our TFP measures need to control for industry differences in any comparison over industries. We do this by creating measures of (log) TFP that are deviations from the industry-by-year average. We refer to this as TFP in the remainder of the paper but it should be interpreted as the deviation of establishment-level TFP from the industry-by-year average.[25]

As noted above, our measure of productivity is a revenue measure of productivity. This means differences in establishment-level prices are embedded in our measure of productivity. Unfortunately, the Census Bureau does not collect establishment-level prices. However, as Foster, Haltiwanger and Syverson (2008) (henceforth FHS) have shown, it is possible to back-out the establishment-level price effects for a limited set of products in Economic Census years (years ending in "2" and "7"). FHS create a physical quantity measure of TFP removing the establishment-level price for establishments producing a set of 11 homogeneous goods (for example, white pan bread). The within-industry correlation between revenue and physical productivity measures in FHS is high (about 0.75). However, FHS also find there is an inverse relationship between physical productivity and prices consistent with establishments facing a differentiated product environment. In addition, FHS find establishment-level prices are positively related to establishment-level demand shocks. As such, our measure of establishment-level productivity should be interpreted as reflecting both technical efficiency and demand factors. More recent work by FHS suggests demand conditions vary substantially by establishment age – and as such the variation in our measure of TFP across establishments of different ages may reflect demand factors more than differences in technical efficiency.[26] However, we only capture the demand factors as they translate into establishment-level prices.

---

[24] As discussed in Syverson (2011), there are numerous alternative ways to measure factor elasticities (e.g., estimation methods using either IV or proxy methods to address endogenous factors). However, as discussed in Syverson (2011), these alternative methods tend to produce similar establishment-level TFP measures (even if they produce somewhat different factor elasticities). Note we have also considered industry-level cost shares averaged over our entire sample and obtain very similar results. Our approach is related to the Divisia/Tornqvist index number approach but it is important to note this latter approach is focused on an index of TFP growth over time. Our focus is on generating a relative productivity measure across establishments within years.
[25] We discuss how we address measurement issues for TFP in greater detail in the Appendix.
[26] See Foster, Haltiwanger and Syverson (2013).

Summary statistics of our integrated establishment-level sample are provided in Table 1. We have roughly 2.2 million establishment-year observations from 1981-2010. We measure growth rates and survival rates for all of these establishments based upon the LBD from t to $t+1$. In Table 1, the growth rate for incumbent establishments is negative.[27] By design, this growth rate does not include the contribution of entry. The growth rate for continuing establishments is about -1 percent and the slightly higher exit rate compared to entry rate implies the overall growth rate is about -2 percent. TFP represents the deviation from industry-year means so by construction has a mean of zero. The within industry-by-year dispersion in TFP is similar to that reported in Syverson (2004). The cyclical variable we focus on (the change in the state-level unemployment rate) has a mean around zero but with substantial variation.[28] It is not uncommon for individual states to experience changes in unemployment of 0.03 in a given year in the Great Recession. About 20 percent of establishments belong to young firms, and the Great Recession dummy applies to less than 10 percent of our establishment-year observations.

We also show summary statistics with establishments classified into young and mature (based upon the age of the firm). We find growth rates for young (excluding startups) are lower than for mature businesses, but this reflects a substantially higher growth rate for continuing young and a substantially higher exit rate for young.

4. Did Reallocation Dynamics Change in the Great Recession?

In this section, we present results of our analysis of the patterns of job creation and job destruction over the cycle. We start by examining job flows for the entire U.S. economy. Panel A of Figure 1 shows the job creation and job destruction rates for the U.S. economy using data from the Business Dynamics Statistics (BDS) series from 1981-2011. The figure also includes a simple cyclical indicator we use frequently in the analysis that follows – namely the change in

---

[27] These statistics use the propensity score weights to adjust the sample, but are not activity weighted.
[28] We use this measure since it is readily available at the national and state level. Moreover, it is highly correlated with measures of national and state level employment growth, GDP growth and with changes in the employment-to-population ratio. For example, at the national level the correlation between GDP growth and the change in the unemployment rate is -0.92, the correlation between the change in the unemployment rate and net employment growth is 0.93, and the correlation between the change in the unemployment rate and the change in the employment-to-population ratio (for the population over age 16) is -0.95. We prefer measures of the cycle that correspond to measures of change and growth as opposed to measures that capture deviations of levels from trends. This preference is because the change and growth measures are much more highly correlated with our outcomes of interest (i.e., employment growth). For example, at the national level the correlation between the Hodrick-Prescott filtered unemployment rate and net employment growth is only -0.23.

the unemployment rate.[29] We start by using the change in the national unemployment rate from the Current Population Survey (CPS). It is apparent that job destruction tends to rise in recessions and job creation tends to fall during periods of increasing unemployment. Interestingly, it appears this pattern changed in the Great Recession. Job destruction did rise sharply in the 2008 to 2009 period, but what is more striking is the sharp fall in job creation that starts in 2007 and persists through 2010. We also note job flows exhibit a downward trend – a point we return to below.

As both a cross check and to explore higher frequency data, we use job creation and destruction series from the Business Employment Dynamics (BED). Panel B of Figure 1 shows quarterly job creation and job destruction rates with the change in the unemployment rate for the period 1990:2 to 2012:1. The quarterly numbers reinforce the message from the annual data that recessions are periods in which job destruction rises and job creation falls. Again, however, job creation falls sharply in 2007 and this persists. The downward trend in the job flows is even more pronounced in the BED. An advantage of the BED is that it is more current: Figure 1B shows the slow recovery from the Great Recession through the first quarter of 2012 is due to anemic job creation rather than job destruction staying persistently high. Other related data sources (e.g., the Job Openings and Labor Turnover Survey, JOLTS) confirm this pattern has continued past the first quarter of 2012.

It is evident from Figure 1 that job creation is as low during the Great Recession as during any period in the last 30 years. Moreover, job reallocation (creation plus destruction) is at its lowest point in 30 years during the Great Recession and its immediate aftermath. For example, job reallocation from the BDS is equal to 28 percent in 2009 (March 2008 to March 2009) even when job destruction peaks – this contrasts with the 35 percent reallocation rate in 1983 (March 1982 to March 1983) when job destruction peaks in the early 1980s recession. These patterns are driven in part by the substantial downward trends in job flows evident in both the BDS and the BED.[30] It is well beyond the scope of this paper to explore the determinants of the declining trends in job flows. See Davis et al. (2007), Decker et al. (2013), and Hyatt and Spletzer (2013) for some efforts in that direction. However, it is clear downward trends are part

---

[29] The change in the unemployment rate is the March-to-March change to match the timing of our job flows series. At the risk of causing confusion, in this section of the paper all measures of growth and change (e.g., job flows and unemployment rate) are measured as percents. In other parts of the paper, such measures are in fractions. We use rates in percents in this section since it facilitates discussion of trends.
[30] Figure E.1 in the Appendix depicts the Hodrick-Prescott trends in the job flows that clearly depict the downward trends.

of the story here, and we need to take the trends into account in our analysis.

To assess the changing pattern of job creation during cyclical downturns, we begin with a simple calculation quantifying the fraction of the changes in net employment accounted for by changes in job creation during periods of net contraction. For each episode of net contraction lasting for one or more periods, we cumulate the net employment losses during the episode (in percentage terms) starting from the beginning of each episode. We also cumulate the change (typically a reduction) in job creation over the same episode. These cumulative changes permit computing the fraction of net employment contraction accounted for by the reduction in job creation.[31] A simple example helps illustrate the calculation. Suppose over four consecutive periods net growth is {0, -4, -6, 0}, job creation is {15, 14, 13, 15} and job destruction is {15, 18, 19, 15}. There is a net contraction during periods 2 and 3. The cumulative net employment decline in periods 2 and 3 is -10 and the cumulative decline in job creation is -3 so the fraction is 0.3.[32]

We sum up these cumulative changes from each cyclical contraction for two sub-periods: pre-Great Recession and post-2007 periods. Then we compute the fraction for each of these changes.[33] Using this cumulative change per episode largely mitigates concerns about trends since the cumulative changes are from the start of each cyclical episode.[34] One limitation of this approach when using the national BDS and BED series is there are a relatively small number of periods over which to make these calculations (the BDS is obviously especially problematic with only 31 total observations). To overcome this limitation, we make this same computation for each state-level job flow series. We then take the average of these fractions across all states.

Table 2 shows the share of the decline in net employment accounted for by declines in job creation during net contractions. We find the share is substantially below 0.5 using the national BDS, the national BED and the state-level BDS for net contractions prior to the pre-Great Recession period. This implies most of the net decline during periods of net contractions before the Great Recession is accounted for by a rise in job destruction rather than a fall in job

---

[31] By construction, overall net contraction is accounted for by the cumulative reductions in job creation and the cumulative increases in job destruction.
[32] Notice it is the cumulative decline in job creation from just prior to the start of the current contraction (that is, the job creation is -1 in period 2 and -2 in period 3 relative to job creation just prior to the start of the current contraction).
[33] This is equivalent to taking the weighted average of the per episode fractions where the weight is the cumulative net change for the episode.
[34] We are cumulating first differences in net employment and job flows – so we are effectively detrending by using first differences.

creation. However, this share rises substantially above 0.5 in the post-2007 period for all three samples. During the Great Recession, most of the net decline is accounted for by a decline in job creation.

We shed further light on these patterns by exploring the relative cyclicality of job creation and destruction pre- and post-2007 taking further advantage of state-level variation. In particular, we consider simple descriptive regressions relating job flows to a cyclical indicator and a dummy variable for the Great Recession period interacted with the cyclical variable. For this purpose, we use state-level changes in the unemployment rate.[35] Since we see a negative trend in job flows, we include a linear trend in our specifications.[36] The results are shown in Table 3. The specifications have a main effect of the cyclical indicator and an interaction effect. As such, the overall effect for the Great Recession is the sum of the main and interaction effect. We find during the Great Recession the relationship between job creation and the change in unemployment becomes more negative, the relationship between job destruction and the change in unemployment becomes less positive and the positive relationship between the reallocation rate and the change in unemployment actually becomes negative.

We also explore the extent to which earlier recessions are different from each other (see Table E.1 in the Appendix). In particular, we estimate specifications equivalent to Table 3 where we include a dummy for the 1981-83 recession interacted with the cyclical indicator as well as the Great Recession dummy interacted with the cyclical indicator as in Table 3.[37] We find no evidence the 1981-83 recession differs from other recessions prior to the Great Recession. Even with this additional dummy, we continue to find the Great Recession is different in a manner very similar to Table 3. Even though these specifications are very simple and intended to be descriptive, note they do allow recessions to differ in their severity and persistence since recessions differ in their patterns of the cyclical indicator. When we find no difference between the 1981-83 recession and other pre-Great Recession contractions, we are not claiming these recessions are the same; but rather that conditional on the severity of the recession, the reallocation patterns are similar. In contrast, the Great Recession is different in its reallocation patterns even taking the severity of the recession into account.

---

[35] We have considered other cyclical indicators such as the change in the employment–to-population ratio (population over age 16) and obtain very similar results.
[36] In unreported results we have found similar patterns using the national sample in spite of the relatively sparse number of observations. We have also found the patterns are robust to using alternative detrending methods.
[37] Here again these are simple specifications with main effects and interaction effects so the overall effect for the early 1980s recession is the main effect plus the interaction effect for the early 1980s recession. The same remarks apply to the Great Recession.

Earlier studies emphasize the large decline in job creation in the Great Recession is driven by a decline in job creation for young and small businesses (see Fort et al., 2013). For ease of exposition, we focus on firm age for this descriptive analysis keeping in mind Fort et al. (2013) find their results for young and small firms hold for young firms since for the most part young firms are small. Defining young firms as those less than 5 years old, Figure 2 shows patterns of job creation and destruction at the *establishment* level by firm age class (young and mature).[38] Job creation fell substantially especially among the very young businesses.[39]

Overall, our evidence points towards the cyclical covariance of job creation and destruction exhibiting different patterns in the Great Recession. Prior to the Great Recession, destruction is more cyclically sensitive and reallocation rises in cyclical downturns. These patterns are consistent with the reallocation timing and cleansing models of Davis and Haltiwanger (1990), Caballero and Hammour (1994) and Mortensen and Pissarides (1994). However, in the Great Recession these patterns changed. Job creation fell much more substantially and job destruction rose less so there is little if any increase in reallocation (the BDS estimates actually yield a decline in reallocation in the Great Recession). The trend decline in job flows also plays a role in these dynamics. The low job creation and reallocation rates in the Great Recession and its aftermath are driven by both trend and cyclical factors.

These patterns do not provide direct information about whether the greater intensity of reallocation in prior recessions was actually productivity enhancing nor whether the slowdown in reallocation in the Great Recession also exhibited changes in the nature of reallocation. To address these questions, we need to explore the relationship between productivity and reallocation.

As a final point for this section, note the patterns we found for the private sector also tend to hold for the manufacturing sector (shown in Appendix Figure E.2). This is relevant since our analysis of the cyclical relationship between productivity and reallocation is confined to the manufacturing sector where we can much more readily measure TFP at the micro level. The different patterns of recessions are especially apparent in comparing the 2001 downturn and the Great Recession. During the 2001 downturn, there was a sharp rise in job destruction with relatively little response of job creation in the manufacturing sector. In contrast, in the Great

---

[38] This analysis is based on establishments classified by the characteristics of the parent firm.
[39] Table E.2 in the Appendix repeats the same type of simple descriptive regressions as in Table 3 by these age categories. We find young businesses have greater sensitivity to the cyclical indicator in terms of both job creation and job destruction. We also find job creation for young businesses fell more with the increase in unemployment in the Great Recession than in prior recessions.

Recession, while job destruction also exhibits a substantial increase, there is a much more notable decline in job creation. When we conduct the same type of exercise as in Table 2 for manufacturing, we find the share of cumulative net losses during contractions accounted for by job creation is equal to 0.13 in contractions prior to the Great Recession and equal to 0.28 post 2007.[40] In manufacturing, variation in job destruction still dominates but variation in job creation plays a substantially larger role in the Great Recession.[41] Even though there are differences in the patterns of the job flows for the entire economy and the manufacturing sector, we think our subsequent analysis of the changing nature of the relationship between productivity and reallocation during the Great Recession using manufacturing establishment-level data has wider relevance. That analysis, to which we now turn, is about the changing relationship between productivity, growth and survival at the micro level – and how that might have changed in the Great Recession.[42]

5. Did Cleansing Effects Change in the Great Recession?

We now address the questions of whether the cleansing effect of recessions is present in our data and in turn whether it changed during the Great Recession. We start by examining the relationship between reallocation and productivity dynamics. Next, we focus on this relationship during recessions to see if we can confirm earlier empirical evidence of a cleansing effect. Finally, we look at whether the cleansing effect of recessions is attenuated during the Great Recession.

Building upon the existing literature concerning the nature of productivity dynamics, we start with a simple regression model linking outcomes to productivity. We focus on the growth and survival dynamics of incumbent establishments. Canonical models of establishment and firm dynamics characterize growth and survival as a function of idiosyncratic and aggregate shocks to productivity and profitability. Establishments with positive idiosyncratic and aggregate shocks are predicted to expand, while establishments with negative shocks are predicted to contract or exit. In the analysis that follows, we use empirical specifications consistent with these models. Our primary focus is on whether there is a connection between productivity enhancing reallocation and the business cycle.

---

[40] We calculate these fractions using periods of net contraction for the overall economy.
[41] Davis and Haltiwanger (1999) show the greater cyclical volatility of job destruction relative to job creation in manufacturing has been present in manufacturing since at least 1947.
[42] In this regard, we note the subsequent analysis abstracts from the trend issues relevant for our analysis with aggregate data since our core specifications at the micro level include year effects (and state effects).

Before proceeding to our analysis of the growth and survival of incumbents, we briefly discuss where entry fits into our analysis. Much of the literature on the role of entry in firm-level productivity dynamics highlights the importance of looking at entrants beyond the point of entry. While the entry point is important, theory and evidence suggest there is a rich "up or out" dynamic for young firms. That is, Jovanovic (1982) type selection and learning dynamics apply primarily to young firms. A complete analysis of entry is beyond the scope of this paper since we are not prepared to explore the determinants of entry in a symmetric way with our exploration of the determinants of growth and survival. To model entry we would need to model potential entrepreneurs – which has been a challenge for the literature both empirically and theoretically. We analyze growth and survival of establishments of young firms separately from those that belong to more mature firms. This analysis of young firms enables us to capture the firm dynamics immediately after entry. Complementing our analysis of the dynamics of young firms, we provide some descriptive analysis of where entrants fall in the productivity distribution at the point of entry. We turn first to the determinants of growth and survival of incumbents.

5.1 Growth and Survival of Incumbents

We look at reallocation on the extensive and intensive margins through empirical specifications relating growth and survival to productivity, the business cycle and their interaction. We consider two samples when looking at establishment growth. First, we look at growth for all (incumbents – that is, they exist in period t) establishments. Second, we consider only establishments that are continuers from t to $t+1$. The use of the DHS growth rate facilitates using both the "all establishments" sample and the "continuing establishments" sample. Recall, with the DHS growth rate, we have a bounded dependent variable and, when using all establishments, we have observations at the lower bound of -2. Likewise, in the exit equation, we use a linear probability specification with the left hand side variable equal to one if exit and zero otherwise.[43] We allow these relationships to vary over the business cycle. Equation (2) shows our basic specification:

---

[43] Haltiwanger, Jarmin and Miranda (2013) explore the implications of using a bounded dependent variable in a similar setting and find results are robust to procedures that are not sensitive to these issues. Moreover, in our case, predicted values of interest are far from the boundaries, which mitigates these concerns.

$$Y_{es,t+1} = \lambda_s + \lambda_{t+1} + \beta * TFP_{est} + \gamma * Cycle_{s,t+1} + \delta * TFP_{est} * Cycle_{s,t+1}$$
$$+ X'_{est}\Theta + \varepsilon_{es,t+1} \qquad (2)$$

where *e* is establishment, *s* is state, *Y* is a set of outcomes, *TFP* is total factor productivity deviations from industry by year means, and *Cycle* is the change in the relevant state unemployment rate from *t* to *t+1*.[44] There are three outcomes (all measured from *t* to *t+1*): "Overall Growth" (continuers+exit), "Exit," and "Conditional Growth" (conditional on survival - i.e., continuers only).[45]

In considering the specification, timing is important. We explore the determinants of growth and survival from *t* to *t+1* based on the productivity of the establishment in period *t* and the business cycle conditions from *t* to *t+1* (we use an indicator of change at the state level – specifically the change in the state level unemployment).

We estimate this specification for 1981-2010 pooling all years with year effects and controlling for establishment characteristics (including establishment size, firm size and state effects).[46] The inclusion of year effects implies we are exploiting state-specific variation in the cycle and that we have abstracted from any of the trend issues (at least national trends) discussed in the previous section. While this is a reduced form specification, it is broadly consistent with the specifications of selection and growth dynamics from the literature. There is already much evidence that high productivity establishments are more likely to survive and grow (see, e.g., Syverson, 2011). Our innovation is to consider how these effects vary over the cycle and in turn across different cycles.

The unit of observation is the establishment in a given state and year, but key right-hand side variables of interest include variables that vary only at the state-year level of aggregation. As such, we cluster the standard errors. We have considered clustering the errors at the state-year

---

[44] We have considered a variety of robustness checks for the cyclical indicator. In Appendix Table E.3, we consider specifications without year effects so that variation in the national cycle is used. In Appendix Table E.4, we consider specifications with year effects but without state effects. In Appendix Table E.5, we report specifications using as the cyclical indicator the change in the employment-to-population (age 16+) ratio. In all cases, results are very similar to those we report in the main text.

[45] One potential limitation of our approach in using outcomes for manufacturing establishments is that they may be less sensitive to local business cycle conditions than establishments in other sectors. We find there is a strong relationship between the outcomes of manufacturing establishments and local business conditions. We note that Syverson (2004) finds many manufactured goods are shipped less than 500 miles. In future work, it would be interesting to consider how the patterns vary by sector (and in turn the local nature of the market for the goods).

[46] For firm size effects, we use firm size classes in period *t*. For establishment size effects, we have considered both establishment size classes and log employment at the establishment level in period *t*. We obtain very similar results for both cases, and in the paper we use log employment at the establishment level.

level and at the state level and obtain similar results. We focus on results using clustering at the state level since Angrist and Pischke (2009) and Arellano (1987) suggest clustering at the state level in related situations has advantages given potential serial correlation in the state-level regressors.

To examine the impact of the Great Recession, we expand Equation (2) to include effects of the Great Recession:

$$Y_{es,t+1} = \lambda_s + \lambda_{t+1} + \beta * TFP_{est} + \gamma * Cycle_{s,t+1} + \delta * TFP_{est} * Cycle_{s,t+1} + \chi * GR_{t+1} * TFP_{est}$$
$$+ \mu * GR_{t+1} * Cycle_{s,t+1} + \phi * GR_{t+1} * Cycle_{s,t+1} * TFP_{est} + X'_{est}\Theta + \varepsilon_{es,t+1} \qquad (3)$$

where GR is a dummy for the Great Recession taking on values of 1 in years 2007-09.[47]

Results of these regressions are shown in Table 4. We first consider specifications without interactions with the Great Recession (columns 1, 3 and 5). In these specifications, the cross-sectional impact of productivity on growth and survival (when the change in the unemployment rate is zero) is given by the first row of columns 1, 3 and 5. Consistent with earlier studies, we find establishment-level productivity is positively related to growth and negatively related to exit in the cross section. All of these effects are statistically significant.

To obtain some perspective on quantitative significance, Figure 3 depicts the implied differences in growth and survival between an establishment one standard deviation below the within industry-year mean and an establishment one standard deviation above the industry-year mean for the main TFP effect (independent of the cycle so Cycle=0). For now, we focus on the bars in Figure 3 labeled "All". Note, Figure 3 also shows how these patterns vary by firm age, and we defer discussion of these effects until later. The difference in overall growth rates between an establishment one standard deviation below and above the mean is about 11 percentage points, the analogous difference in exit rates is 4 percentage points, and the difference in the growth of survivors is 3 percentage points. Comparing the magnitudes of the difference for overall growth with the difference for conditional growth, it is evident the predicted difference in overall growth rates is largely accounted for by the predicted difference in exit rates.[48]

Returning to Table 4, we also find growth and survival of manufacturing establishments

---

[47] GR indicates outcomes from March 2007 to March 2010.
[48] Note the "exit" outcome in Table 4 and Figure 3 is from a linear probability model so that there is no simple aggregation of the survival growth and exit outcomes to obtain the overall growth outcome. This requires translating exit into job destruction from exit. The difference between the overall growth and survival growth yields an estimate of the latter (appropriately weighting survival growth for the share of continuing establishments).

are related to local business cycle conditions. Increases in the state-level unemployment rate are associated with declines in growth and increases in exit. All of these effects are statistically significant and large in magnitude.

Of primary interest, we find the relationship between productivity and reallocation is enhanced in business cycle contractions. The positive impact of productivity on overall growth and negative impact of productivity on exit are both increased in magnitude during periods with increases in state-level unemployment. Both of these effects are large in magnitude and statistically significant. We find the point estimate for this interaction effect is positive for the growth of continuing establishments, but is not statistically significant at conventional levels. As we discuss below, this is sensitive to permitting effects to vary with firm age.

Did these patterns change in the Great Recession? Columns 2, 4 and 6 of Table 4 speak to this question. We are particularly interested in the interaction effect of TFP and the cycle. First, we find the magnitude of the estimated interaction effect between TFP and the cycle is larger for the period prior to the Great Recession than what we find in columns 1, 3 and 5 when we pool all recessions together. This pattern is especially notable for the overall growth and exit specifications. Driving this is the estimated 3-way interaction between TFP, the cycle and the Great Recession which is reported in the last row of columns 2, 4, and 6. For overall growth, we find the 3-way estimated effect is negative and statistically significant. Observe as well the magnitude of the overall interaction between TFP and the cycle is negative in the Great Recession (adding together the 2.182 and -2.961). Thus, instead of the cycle enhancing the impact of TFP on overall growth, it tends to diminish it on the margin. A similar pattern is observed for exit. The estimated 3-way interaction effect is positive and larger in magnitude than the 2-way interaction effect of TFP and the cycle. Instead of the cycle enhancing the impact of TFP on exit, it tends to diminish it on the margin. For growth of continuing establishments, we find less systematic patterns. It appears the 3-way interaction for overall growth is being driven mostly by the exit margin.

There are other estimated interactions of interest in columns 2, 4 and 6. In particular, we find the impact of the cycle is even more severe in terms of its impact on growth and survival in the Great Recession. We also find the main effects of TFP (independent of the cycle) on growth and survival are slightly enhanced in the Great Recession (although only statistically significant for exit).

We use the same type of exercise as in Figure 3 to quantify how the relationship between productivity, growth and survival changes with the cycle. Figure 4 depicts such exercises for the overall growth and exit outcomes of all establishments. We focus on overall growth and survival since we obtain statistically significant effects for the interaction between the effects of TFP and the cycle for these outcomes.[49] The leftmost bar labeled "Normal" (zero change in unemployment) is taken from Figure 3. The remaining bars of each figure show how these outcomes vary with the cycle. Mild contraction is a 1 percentage point increase in state-level unemployment, sharp contraction is a 3 percentage point increase in state-level unemployment, and GR is for the period 2007-09 (reflecting outcomes from March 2007 to March 2010).

We find the difference in overall growth between high and low productivity establishments increases substantially when unemployment rises in periods before the Great Recession. In a sharp contraction (increase in unemployment of 3 percentage points), the difference in overall growth rates exceeds 15 percentage points (see Figure 4A). The Great Recession modifies these patterns. The difference in growth rates between high and low productivity establishments is still large in the Great Recession but rather than increasing with unemployment, it falls with increases in unemployment. In a mild contraction (increase in unemployment of 1 percentage point) in the Great Recession, the difference in growth rates between high and low productivity establishments is about 13 percentage points. For a sharp contraction, this falls to about 12 percentage points.

Closely related patterns are exhibited in Figure 4B for the exit margin. In cyclical contractions before the Great Recession, the difference in exit rates between low and high productivity establishments rises with larger increases in unemployment (note that in Figure 4B we use the difference in exit rates between *low* and *high* productivity establishments). However, in the Great Recession, this pattern reverses. While there is still a substantially higher probability of exit of low productivity businesses during the Great Recession, this difference declines with larger increases in unemployment.[50]

We now turn to exploring whether these patterns vary by firm age. We categorize establishments in terms of the age of the parent firm to build on the insights of Fort et al. (2013) and FHS (2013). Fort et al. (2013) find establishments belonging to young and small firms are hit especially hard in the Great Recession. FHS (2013) find young establishments in manufacturing take a long time to break into their respective industry and geographic markets. We denote as

---

[49] For completeness, we show the results for continuing establishments in Appendix Figure E.3.
[50] In Appendix Table E.6 we show the results in Table 4 are broadly similar if we exclude the 1981-83 recession suggesting our results are not simply driven by differences between the 1981-83 recession and the Great Recession.

"Young" establishments that are part of young firms and call the remaining establishments of mature firms, "Mature".[51] In what follows, unless otherwise specified, when we say young (mature) establishments we are referring to establishments from young (mature) firms. While we acknowledge this approach is indirect and at best suggestive, exploring the role of firm age in this context can shed light on the impact of the financial collapse of the Great Recession to the extent young firms were more adversely impacted by this collapse.

The results of these regressions are shown in Table 5. We find that the general patterns for the full sample hold for both "Young" and "Mature" (compare columns 1, 3 and 5 in Table 5 to those in Table 4). However, the quantitative magnitudes are substantially larger for the establishments of young firms. To see this, we start by returning to Figure 3. For young businesses, we find that the difference in growth rates for an establishment one standard deviation below and above mean productivity is about 17 percentage points. In contrast, the analogous difference for mature establishments is about 10 percentage points. The exit and growth rate of continuers for young establishments are also substantially more sensitive to productivity than mature establishments.

Table 5 shows establishments of young firms are also more sensitive to the cycle, and the interaction effect of the cycle and productivity is larger in magnitude for establishments of young firms and is statistically significant for all three outcomes. The significance of the estimated 2-way interaction between TFP and the cycle for the growth of continuing young establishments is especially notable since it contrasts with the results of Table 4 where we could not detect a statistically significant relationship. Table 5 helps account for this as we find that the 2-way interaction effect between TFP and the cycle is actually negative (although not significant) for mature continuing establishments. Apparently, cleansing effects on this margin (growth of continuing establishments) are only present for young businesses.

Did these patterns change in the Great Recession? For the 3-way interaction effect of interest between TFP, the cycle and the Great Recession, we find point estimates largely consistent with those for the full sample but with less systematic statistical significance. Part of the challenge here is that the number of establishments from young firms is only about 20 percent of the overall sample and the 3-way interactions are focusing on a specific 3-year period (2007-09). Based on the point estimates for establishments of young firms, we find that the 3-way interaction effect between TFP, the cycle and the Great Recession tends to offset the 2-way

---

[51] Results are similar when we use measures of "Young" that rely on establishment age.

interaction effect between TFP and the cycle. But while the patterns are systematic, they are not precisely estimated. For mature establishments, we find smaller 3-way interaction estimates but they still tend to systematically offset the 2-way interaction of TFP and the cycle. We know from Table 4 that when pooled we obtain large, statistically significant effects for the 3-way interaction that offset the 2-way interaction. We are pushing the data pretty hard in seeking to identify differential 3-way interaction effects by firm age – especially given the group that is more sensitive to the cycle (young) has relatively small samples for the 2007-09 period.

We illustrate the predictions from Table 5 in Figure 5 in the same manner as Figure 4. We focus on overall growth for the sake of brevity.[52] Figure 5 shows the differences in growth rates between high and low productivity establishments are much larger for establishments of young as opposed to mature firms. For example, in Figure 5 the difference in growth rates between high and low productivity establishments of young firms is over 15 percentage points while the difference for establishments of mature firms is generally around 10 percentage points. This differential grows for both young and mature but especially for young during periods of rising unemployment prior to the Great Recession. For young, it grows to over 25 percent in a sharp contraction. During the Great Recession, this differential is only at 21 percent for a sharp contraction. While appropriate caution is needed for the latter interaction with the Great Recession given the lack of statistical precision, it still suggests earlier results about the Great Recession being less productivity enhancing is being driven disproportionately by young establishments.

5.2 Where Do Entrants Fit In?

The analysis above focuses on the determinants of growth and survival of incumbent establishments and does not directly consider entry. However, we have some indirect analysis in our breakdown of establishments into "Young" and "Mature." We find there are larger effects of productivity, the cycle and the interaction of the two for young as opposed to mature businesses. The specifications of growth and survival we use in the prior section, while not derived explicitly from a structural model, are consistent with theoretical models of firm dynamics in the literature. The equivalent for entry would seek to capture the decision rules of potential entrants, which is well beyond the scope of the current paper. While we do not pursue this path, we can conduct a

---

[52] Appendix Figures E.4 and E.5 show the results for exit and growth of continuing establishments respectively. The much larger response of young continuing establishments to TFP and to the interaction of TFP and the cycle is evident in Figure E.5.

simple descriptive analysis of where entrants fit relative to incumbents in terms of the productivity distribution and how this changes over the cycle.

For this purpose, we estimate a simple descriptive linear probability specification based upon classifying establishments in any given year into two groups: new entrants (those establishments for whom this is the first year of operation) and existing establishments (those establishments who have activity in prior years).

The specification has as the left-hand side variable *entry* equal to one if the establishment is a new entrant and equal to zero otherwise. On the right-hand side, we include TFP in the current year, a measure of the *Cycle* (in this case from t-1 to t since the designation of entry is for establishments that entered between t-1 and t), and the interaction. We also include a specification where we permit these relationships to differ in the Great Recession using a *GR* dummy (again being careful to treat the timing differently since this outcome is between t-1 and t).

We report results for this descriptive regression in Table 6. We find higher productivity establishments are slightly less likely to be entrants. The estimated effect is statistically significant given our sample size but is quantitatively small. Moving from one standard deviation below the (within industry) mean to one standard deviation above mean implies a difference in the likelihood of being an entrant of less than half a percent. Thus entrants have slightly lower productivity than incumbents. This finding is consistent with findings in Foster, Haltiwanger and Krizan (2001) and FHS (2008). In terms of FHS (2008), recall this pattern may reflect lower prices for entrants compared to incumbents (given our TFP measure is a measure of TFPR rather than TFPQ).

Not surprisingly, the likelihood an establishment is an entrant is lower in times of rising unemployment in the state. In terms of the interaction between TFP and the cycle, we find a positive and significant point estimate suggesting entrants in contractions are relatively more productive than in expansions. Again, however, this effect is relatively small. For an increase in unemployment of 3 percentage points, the probability a high productivity establishment is an entrant is actually positive but very small. Moving from one standard deviation below mean productivity to one standard deviation above mean productivity yields a one tenth of one percent higher probability that an establishment is an entrant (during a period of a sharp contraction). We find little evidence these patterns changed substantially in the Great Recession (i.e., even at point estimates the effects remain small). We know from earlier work (e.g., Fort et al., 2013) that job creation from entry fell substantially in the Great Recession. This is not inconsistent with the patterns here given the large negative coefficient on the cyclical variable. It is a bit surprising that the interaction between GR and the cycle is not statistically significant (although it is negative, consistent with earlier work).

5.3 Aggregate Implications

The analysis of the relationship between productivity and reallocation above is based on the relationship between growth, survival and productivity at the establishment level. A strength of this approach is the rich set of controls we are able to use while focusing on within state variation in the cycle over time to identify the effects of interest. A limitation of the analysis is that it is difficult to draw inferences about aggregate consequences for productivity. A full analysis of the latter is beyond the scope of this paper but in this section we conduct a counterfactual exercise we think sheds light on the aggregate consequences.

Much of the literature on the aggregate relationship between productivity and reallocation (see Syverson (2011) for a recent survey) revolves around the extent to which resources are shifted away from less productive to more productive establishments. Our micro analysis is very much about such shifts, a fact which we now exploit in a simple counterfactual exercise. Following the spirit of the accounting decompositions in Foster, Haltiwanger and Krizan (2001) and Foster, Haltiwanger and Syverson (2008), we consider the following exercise. Our data permits quantifying the relationship between the size distribution of establishments and productivity (within industries) in any given year. Our micro-econometric analysis enables us to predict employment growth and survival based on the interaction of productivity and cyclical effects. We use the estimated model to generate a counterfactual distribution of employment based on the initial conditions of productivity, employment and the cycle.[53] For the latter, we exploit the variation in the estimates we have detected for downturns prior to the Great Recession and during the Great Recession. To gauge the aggregate implications, we compare the difference between employment-weighted average productivity in the base year and employment-weighted average productivity using the counterfactual distribution of employment. Since we use productivity measured as deviations from within industry-by-year means, this calculation yields an estimate of the implied increase in within industry productivity from reallocation effects alone. In making this calculation we ignore the contribution of entry since the

---

[53] We use the estimates from the overall growth model for this exercise.

analysis above suggests entrants tend to come in close to the mean in the first year of entry.[54]

Figure 6 shows the results of this exercise. The bar labeled "Normal" implies that in a year with no change in the unemployment rate, the average increase in productivity from reallocation effects from one year to the next across incumbents is about 2.1 log points.[55] During Mild and Sharp contractions prior to the Great Recession, this contribution increases to 2.4 and 2.9 log points respectively. But during the Great Recession, during Mild and Sharp contractions (which can be thought of as the effect across different states) the reallocation contribution is 2.3 and 2.1 log points respectively. Consistent with our micro evidence, the contribution of reallocation to this aggregate index of establishment-level productivity decreases in the Great Recession.

These estimates of the contribution of reallocation are large relative to those in the literature. In accounting decompositions such as those in Foster, Haltiwanger and Krizan (2001) and Foster, Haltiwanger and Syverson (2008), reallocation effects account for up to half of industry-level productivity growth using similar activity-weighted establishment-level productivity as indices of industry-level productivity. In these papers, this type of average industry index grows by about 1 log point per year so that half of this is substantially below the greater than 2 log point effects we are capturing. However, a strength of our current approach relative to this existing literature is that our counterfactual exercise focuses on the reallocation effects induced by productivity differences. That is, in this earlier literature, the accounting decompositions capture the contribution of reallocation of activity across establishments regardless of the source of that reallocation. The work of Foster, Haltiwanger and Syverson (2008, 2013) emphasizes that much reallocation is induced by demand side effects as opposed to productivity effects. Our TFPR captures some but hardly all of the demand side effects identified in this recent work. Instead, our counterfactual exercise is based on the reallocation that is directly linked to productivity differences (as measured by TFPR). Taking our results at face

---

[54] We can make these calculations for any given year since they depend on the joint distribution of employment and productivity in the base year. We make these calculations for every year and then report the difference between counterfactual and base year averaged across all years.

[55] The index of productivity we use here is an employment-weighted average of establishment-level productivity. In this respect it is related to the indices used in Baily, Hulten and Campbell (1992), Olley and Pakes (1996) and Foster, Haltiwanger and Krizan (2001). Much of the work using activity-weighted averages of establishment-level TFP uses either output or composite input weights. We do not have that information for our counterfactual (we use the LBD to generate outcome measures for the counterfactual) so we are restricted to using the activity measures in our outcome measures – namely employment. Foster, Haltiwanger and Krizan (2001) show these activity-weighted indices are similar using output, input or employment weights. The interpretation with employment weights is that this is an index of TFP for the average unit of employment.

value yields a substantial contribution to productivity growth from productivity difference induced reallocation.[56]

6. Conclusions and Future Work

We address the question "Was the Great Recession a cleansing recession?" by building up five related facts. First, we show reallocation in the Great Recession differs markedly from earlier recessions. Job creation falls much more substantially than in prior recessions and job destruction rises less than in prior recessions – taken together they yield less of an increase (or even a decline) in the intensity of reallocation. Second, we find reallocation is productivity enhancing. Less productive establishments are more likely to exit, while more productive establishments are more likely to grow. Third, we show these patterns are enhanced in recessions prior to the Great Recession. Fourth, we show reallocation is less productivity enhancing in the Great Recession as contractions become more severe. The gap in growth rates and exit rates between high productivity and low productivity businesses decreases rather than increases with larger increases in unemployment in the Great Recession. Fifth, we find that the implied increases in aggregate (industry-level) productivity indices from productivity-induced reallocation are substantial, with even larger effects in sharp contractions prior to the Great Recession and smaller effects in sharp contractions in the Great Recession.

Our analysis is mostly descriptive – evaluating how the patterns and nature of reallocation change over the cycle and how they differ in the Great Recession. We do not directly address why the Great Recession is different. As such, our contribution is much more about what happened than why it happened. The obvious next step is to explore why the patterns are different. A clear candidate is the role of the financial collapse. Our finding that the patterns change more for young businesses is at least suggestive that the financial collapse (which arguably hit young firms much harder) is relevant. But to provide convincing evidence, we need to find ways to integrate direct measures of the financial collapse at the firm or at least regional level into the type of analysis we have conducted here.[57]

---

[56] We note our counterfactual exercise is not well suited to provide a full accounting of overall industry level productivity growth. For example, our data is not well suited to capture the within establishment productivity growth that is a critical part of the overall growth. We are using the high frequency ASM data which is well suited for measuring the cross sectional distribution of TFP within industries in a given year but less well suited to measure within establishment productivity growth given the sample limitations of the ASM.

[57] Fort et al. (2013) present evidence that the fall in housing prices is important for understanding the especially large decline of young businesses in the Great Recession.

This paper raises questions which bear looking into in future research. One interesting question concerns heterogeneity of recessions in general. In comparing the Great Recession to earlier recessions in our productivity analysis, we group all of the earlier recessions for which we have data into one category in our main analysis. Much of the thinking about cleansing recessions was motivated by the patterns seen in the 1981-83 recession. The 1981-83 recession has a big surge in destruction and exits of low productivity establishments followed by a big surge in creation as early as 1984. That recession is very different from the relatively mild recessions of 1991 and 2001.[58] We do sensitivity analysis that suggests our results are not driven by the differences between the 1981-83 recession and the Great Recession, but there is much room for further research in this area. In particular, investigating differences across recessions taking into account the different driving forces of recessions would be a promising area for future research. This would be one way to help understand why the Great Recession looks different in terms of its reallocation dynamics.

Another interesting area for future research is to explore the implications of the declining trend in job flows exhibited in the U.S. over the last few decades for productivity growth. Both the BDS and BED show pronounced downward trends in job flows and thus the pace of reallocation. Since we find reallocation is productivity enhancing in general (ignoring the cycle), the obvious question is whether this has implications for long run trend productivity growth in the U.S.

Finally, we note a core limitation of our current analysis is that we study the relationship between productivity and reallocation only for the manufacturing sector. While manufacturing is interesting and important, much of the changing patterns of job reallocation in terms of trends and the cycle are driven by other sectors. Our focus on manufacturing is driven by data limitations. There are sources that can be used for measuring productivity (even TFP) for establishments and firms in other sectors – but this will require addressing a variety of challenges in terms of measurement and methodology. The high pace of reallocation in non-manufacturing sectors and the changing patterns of reallocation suggest addressing such challenges would have substantial payoffs.

---

[58] Our descriptive analysis in Section 5 shows these shallower recessions did not differ much from the early 1980s recession in terms of the covariance between job flows and the cycle. The 1991 and 2001 recessions differ in terms of the severity of the recessions but the covariance between job flows and changes in unemployment are similar across the 1981-83, 1991 and 2001 recessions.

References

Angrist, Joshua and Jorn-Steffen Pischke. 2009. *Mostly Harmless Econometrics*. Princeton: Princeton University Press.

Arellano, Manuel. 1987. Computing Robust Standard Errors for Within-Group Estimators. *Oxford Bulletin of Economics and Statistics* 49, pp. 431-34.

Baily, Martin Neil, Eric J. Bartelsman, and John Haltiwanger. 2001. Labor Productivity: Structural Change and Cyclical Dynamics. *Review of Economics and Statistics* 83, no. 3: 420-33.

Baily, Martin Neil, Charles Hulten, and David Campbell. 1992. Productivity Dynamics in Manufacturing Plants. In *Brookings Papers on Economic Activity: Microeconomics*, ed. Clifford Winston and Martin Neil Baily. Washington, DC: Brookings Institution Press.

Barlevy, Gadi. 2003. Credit Market Frictions and the Allocation of Resources over the Business Cycle. *Journal of Monetary Economics* 50, no. 8: 1795-1818.

Barlevy, Gadi. 2002. The Sullying Effect of Recessions. *The Review of Economic Studies* 69, no. 1: 65-96.

Bartelsman, Eric J. and Mark Doms. 2000. Understanding Productivity: Lessons from Longitudinal Microdata. *Journal of Economic Literature* 38, no. 3: 569-95.

Bernanke, Ben and Mark Gertler. 1989. Agency Costs, Net Worth, and Business Fluctuations. *The American Economic Review* 79, no. 1: 14-31.

Blanchard, Oliver Jean and Peter Diamond. 1990. The Cyclical Behavior of the Gross Flows of U.S. Workers. In *Brookings Papers on Economic Activity 2*, ed. William C. Brainard and George L. Perry. Washington, DC: Brookings Institution Press.

Bloom, Nicholas, Erik Brynjolfsson, Lucia Foster, Ron Jarmin, Itay Saporta-Eksten, and John Van Reenen. 2013. Management in America. CES-WP-13-01, CES Discussion Paper Series, Washington, DC.

Caballero, Ricardo J. and Mohamad L. Hammour. 1994. The Cleansing Effect of Recessions. *The American Economic Review* 84, no. 5: 1350-68.

Caballero, Ricardo J. and Mohamad L. Hammour. 1996. On the Timing and Efficiency of Creative Destruction. *Quarterly Journal of Economics* 111, no. 3: 805-32.

Caballero, Ricardo J. and Mohamad L. Hammour. 2005. The Cost of Recessions Revisited: A Reverse-Liquidationist View. *The Review of Economic Studies* 72, no. 2: 313-41.

Campbell, Jeffrey R. 1998. Entry, Exit, and Embodied Technology, and Business Cycles. *Review of Economic Dynamics* 1, no. 2: 371-408.

Collard-Wexler, Alan and Jan De Loecker. 2013. Reallocation and Technology: Evidence from the U.S. Steel Industry. Working Paper no. 18739, National Bureau of Economic Research, Cambridge, MA.

Davis, Steven, R. Jason Faberman, and John Haltiwanger. 2006. The Flow Approach to Labor Markets: New Data Sources and Micro-Macro Links. *Journal of Economic Perspectives* 20, no. 3:3-26.

Davis, Steven, R. Jason Faberman, and John Haltiwanger. 2012. Labor Market Flows in the Cross Section and Over Time. *Journal of Monetary Economics* 59, no. 1: 1-18.

Davis, Steven J. and John Haltiwanger. 1990. Gross Job Creation and Destruction: Microeconomic Evidence and Macroeconomic Implications. In *NBER Macroeconomics Annual 1990*, ed. Olivier Jean Blanchard and Stanley Fischer. Cambridge, MA: MIT Press.

Davis, Steven J. and John Haltiwanger. 1992. Gross Job Creation, Gross Job Destruction, and Employment Reallocation. *The Quarterly Journal of Economics* 107, no. 3: 819-63.

Davis, Steven J. and John Haltiwanger. 1999. On the Driving Forces Behind Cyclical Movements in Employment and Job Reallocation. *American Economic Review* 89, no. 5: 1234-58.

Davis, Steven J., John C. Haltiwanger, and Scott Schuh. 1996. *Job Creation and Destruction.* Cambridge MA: MIT Press.

Davis Steven J., John Haltiwanger, Ron Jarmin and Javier Miranda, 2007. Volatility and Dispersion in Business Growth Rates: Publicly Traded versus Privately Held Firms. In *NBER Macroeconomics Annual 2006*, ed. Daron Acemoglu, Kenneth Rogoff, and Michael Woodford. Cambridge, MA: MIT Press.

Decker, Ryan, John Haltiwanger, Ron Jarmin and Javier Miranda. 2013. The Secular Decline in Business Dynamism in the U.S. Unpublished manuscript.

Dunne, Timothy. 1998. CES Data Issues Memorandum, 98:1. Center for Economic Studies, U.S. Census Bureau.

Ericson, Richard and Ariel Pakes. 1995. Markov-Perfect Industry Dynamics: A Framework for Empirical Work. *The Review of Economic Studies* 62, no. 1: 53-82.

Eslava, Marcela, Arturo Galindo, Marc Hofstetter, Alejandro Izquierdo. 2010. Scarring Recessions and Credit Constraints: Evidence from Colombian Firm Dynamics. ISSN 1657-5334, Documentos CEDE.

Fort, Teresa, John Haltiwanger, Ron S. Jarmin, and Javier Miranda. 2013. How Firms Respond to Business Cycles: The Role of Firm Age and Firm Size. *IMF Economic Review*, 1-40.

Foster, Lucia, John Haltiwanger, and Chad Syverson. 2008. Reallocation, Firm Turnover, and Efficiency: Selection on Productivity or Profitability? *American Economic Review* 98, no. 1: 394-425.

Foster, Lucia, John Haltiwanger, and Chad Syverson. 2013. The Slow of Growth of New Plants: Learning about Demand. Working Paper no. 17853, National Bureau of Economic Research, Cambridge, MA.

Foster, Lucia, John Haltiwanger, and C.J. Krizan. 2001. Market Selection, Reallocation and Restructuring in the U.S. Retail Trade Sector in the 1990s. In *New Directions in Productivity Analysis*, ed. Edward Dean, Michael Harper and Charles Hulten. Chicago and London: University of Chicago Press.

Foster, Lucia, John Haltiwanger, and C.J. Krizan. 2006. Aggregate Productivity Growth: Lessons from Microeconomic Evidence. *Review of Economics and Statistics* 88, no. 4: 748-58.

Griliches, Zvi and Haim Regev. 1995. Productivity and Firm Turnover in Israeli Industry: 1979-1988. *Journal of Econometrics* 65, no. 1: 175-203.

Haltiwanger, John, Ron Jarmin and Javier Miranda. 2011. Historically Large Decline in Job Creation from Startups and Existing Firms in the 2008-09 Recession. Brief no. 5, Kauffman Foundation Business Dynamics Statistics Briefing, Kansas City, MO.

Haltiwanger, John and Ron Jarmin and Javier Miranda. 2013. Who Creates Jobs? Small vs. Large vs. Young. *Review of Economic and Statistics*, 95, no. 2: forthcoming.

Hopenhayn, Hugo. 1992. Entry, Exit, and Firm Dynamics in Long Run Equilibrium. *Econometrica* 60, no. 5: 1127-50.

Hopenhayn, Hugo and Richard Rogerson. 1993. Job Turnover and Policy Evaluation: A General Equilibrium Analysis. *Journal of Political Economy* 101, no. 5: 915-38.

Hyatt, Henry and James Spletzer. 2013. The Recent Decline in Employment Dynamics. CES-WP-13-03, Center for Economic Studies Working Paper, Washington, DC.

Jarmin, Ron S. and Javier Miranda. 2002. The Longitudinal Business Database. CES-WP-02-17, Center for Economic Studies Working Paper, Washington, DC.

Jovanovic, Boyan. 1982. Selection and the Evolution of Industry. *Econometrica* 50, no. 3: 649-70.

Lee, Yoonsoo and Toshihiko Mukoyama. 2012. Entry, Exit, and Plant-level Dynamics over the Business Cycle.

Mortensen, Dale T., and Christopher A. Pissarides. 1994. Job Creation and Job Destruction and the Theory of Unemployment. *Review of Economic Studies* LXI, no. 3:397-415.

Olley, Steven and Ariel Pakes. 1996. The Dynamics of Productivity in the Telecommunications Equipment Industry. *Econometrica* 64, no. 6: 1263-1310.

Osotimehin, Sophie and Francesco Pappadà. 2013. Credit Frictions and the Cleansing Effect of Recessions. Unpublished manuscript, University of Virginia, Charlottesville.

Ouyang, Min. 2009. The Scarring Effect of Recessions. *Journal of Monetary Economics* 56, no. 2: 184-99.

Roberts, Mark J., and Dylan Supina. 1996. Output Price, Markups, and Producer Size. *European Economic Review*, 40(3), 909-921.

Schumpeter, Joseph A. 1939. *Business Cycles: A Theoretical, Historical and Statistical Analysis of the Capitalist Process*. 2 vols. New York: McGraw Hill.

Schumpeter, Joseph A. 1942. *Capitalism, Socialism and Democracy*. New York: Harper.

Syverson, Chad. 2004. Product Substitutability and Productivity Dispersion. *Review of Economics and Statistics* 86, no. 2: 534-50

Syverson, Chad. 2011. "What Determines Productivity?" *Journal of Economic Literature* 49, no. 2: 326-65.

Tornqvist, Leo, Pentti Vartia and Yrjo Vartia, 1985, "How Should Relative Changes Be Measured?" *American Statistician*, February, 39:1, pp. 43-46.

Figure 1. Job Flows and the Business Cycle

A. Annual, 1981-2011

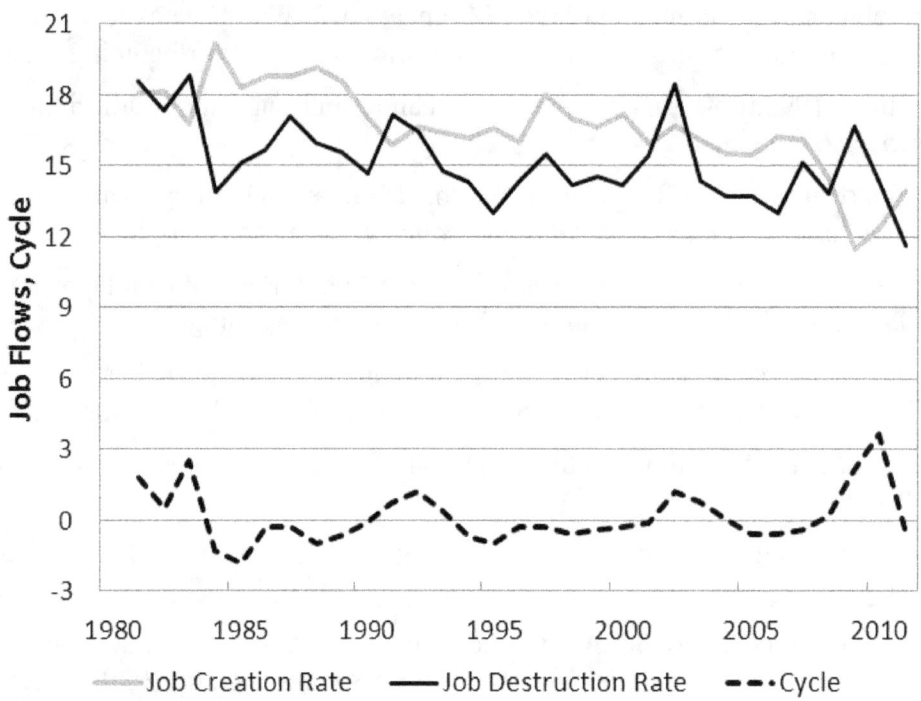

B. Quarterly, 1990:2-2012:1

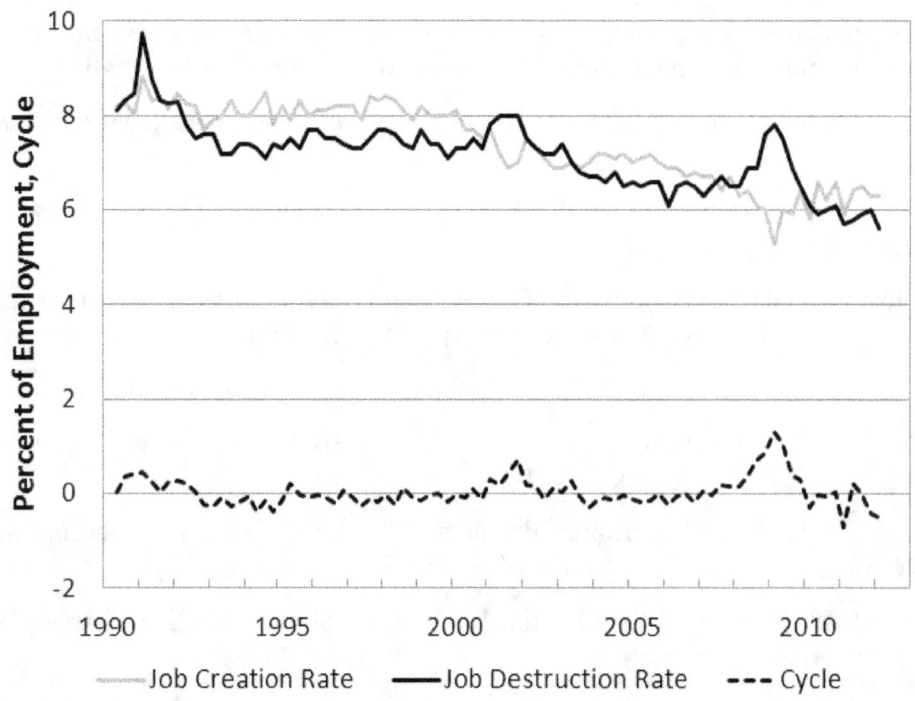

Source: Authors calculations using the BDS (Annual), BED (Quarterly) and CPS.

Note: Cycle is the change in the unemployment rate.

Figure 2. Job Flows by Age, 1981-2011

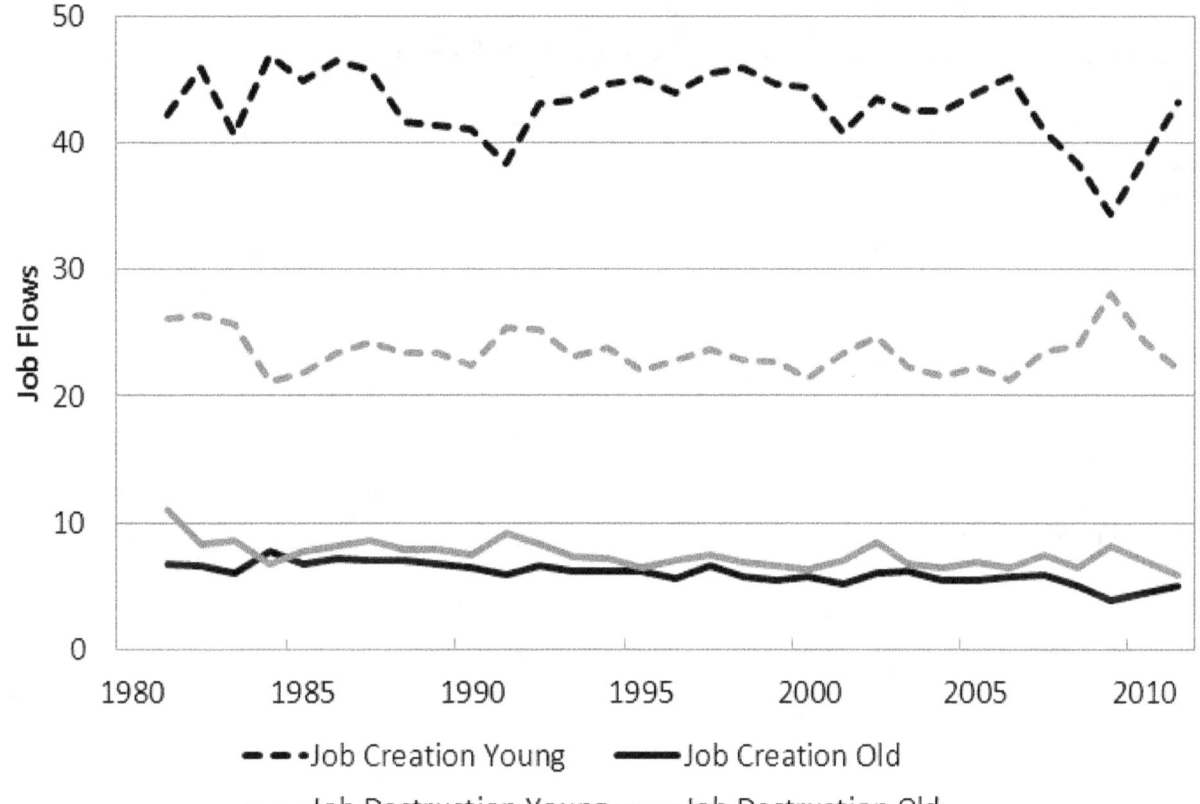

Source: Authors' calculations on the BDS.

Notes:
1. Young is for establishments owned by firms less than 5 years old. Mature is for establishments owned by firms 5 or more years old.
2. Job flows are establishment-based and are classified by firm age characteristics.

Figure 3. Differences in Growth Rates Between High and Low Productivity Establishments, Normal Times

Panel A. Overall Growth (Continuing + Exiting Establishments)

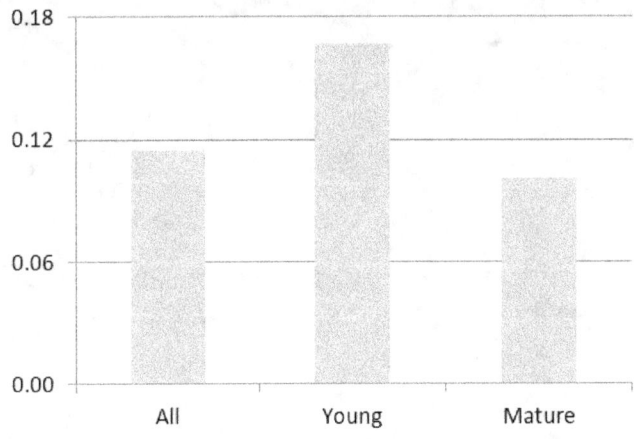

Panel B. Exit Rates

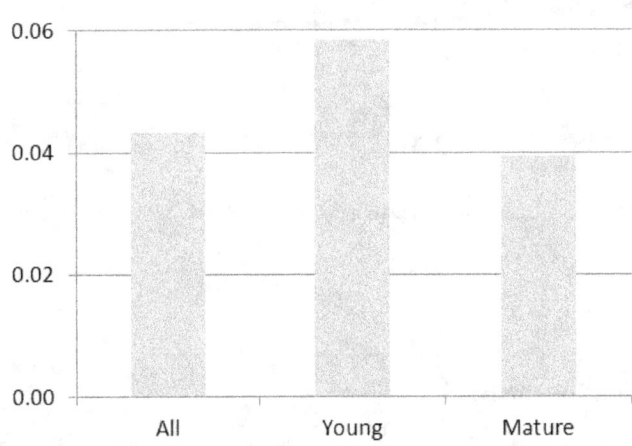

Panel C. Conditional Growth (Continuers Only)

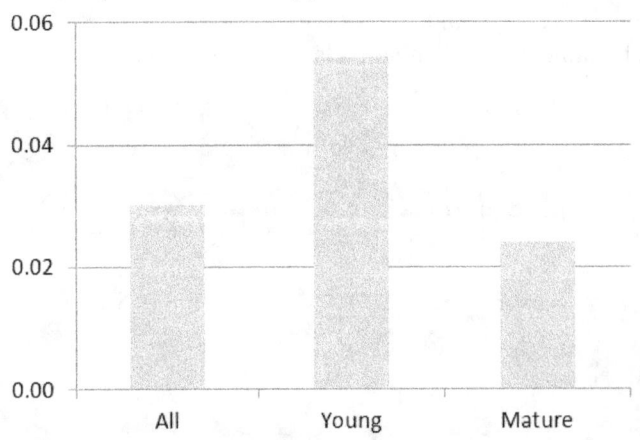

Source: Authors' calculations on the ASM, CM and LBD.

Depicted is the predicted difference in growth rates (panels A and C, high minus low) and the predicted difference in probability of exit (panel B, low minus high) between an establishment one standard deviation above industry-by-year mean productivity and an establishment one standard deviation below industry-by-year mean productivity. Normal is zero change in state-level unemployment.

Figure 4. Differences in Growth and Exit Rates Between High and Low Productivity Establishments Over the Business Cycle

Panel A. Overall Growth and Productivity (Continuing + Exiting Establishments)

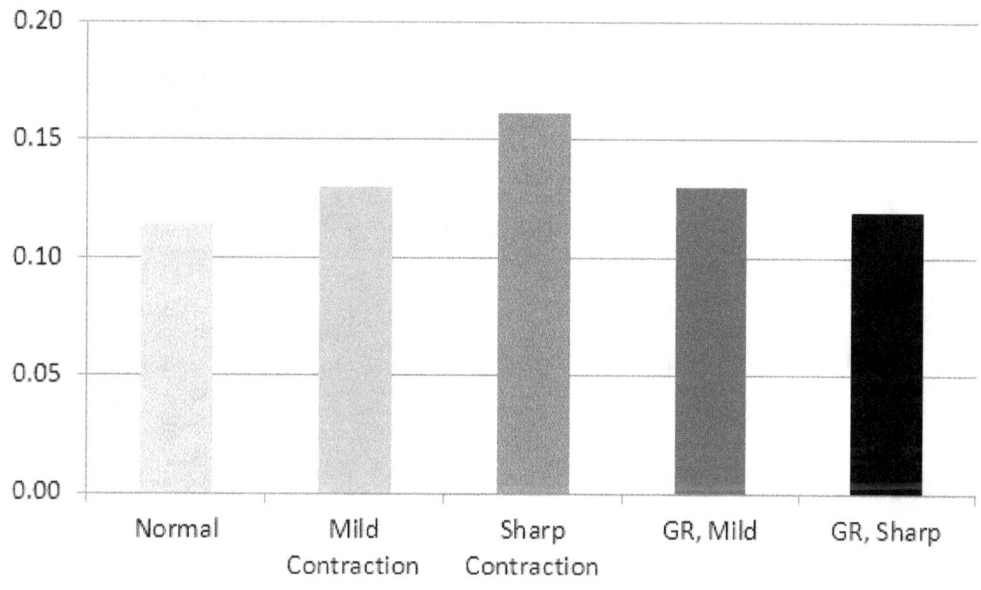

Panel B. Exit Rates

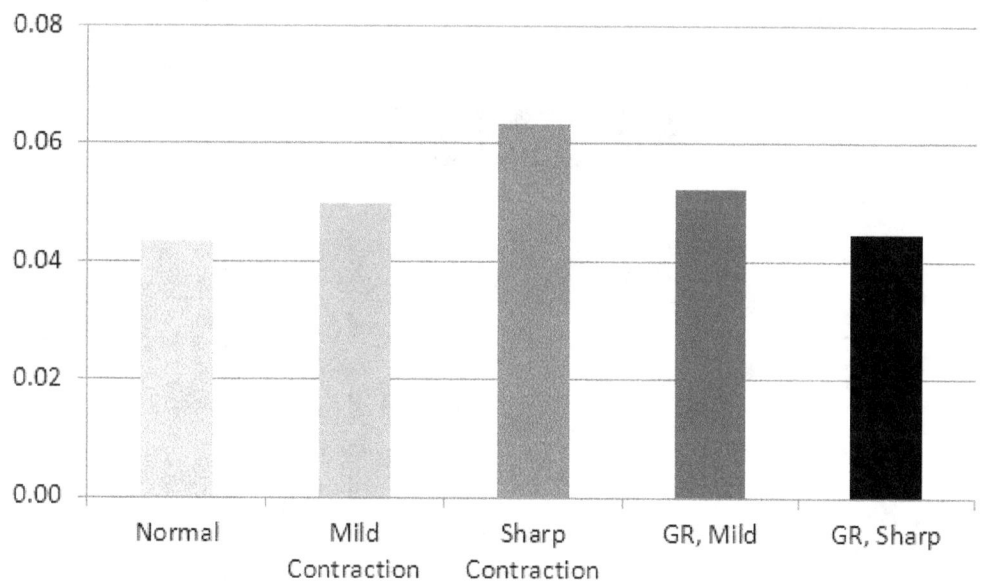

Source: Authors' calculations on the ASM, CM and LBD.

Notes: Depicted is the predicted difference in growth rates (panel A, high minus low) and the predicted difference in probability of exit (panel B, low minus high) between an establishment one standard deviation above industry-by-year mean productivity and an establishment one standard deviation below industry-by-year mean productivity. Normal is zero change in state-level unemployment, mild contraction is 1 percentage point increase in state level unemployment, sharp contraction is 3 percentage point increase in state-level unemployment, GR is for period 2007-09.

Figure 5. Differences in Overall Growth Rates (Continuing + Exiting Establishments) Between High and Low Productivity Establishments Over the Business Cycle: By Firm Age

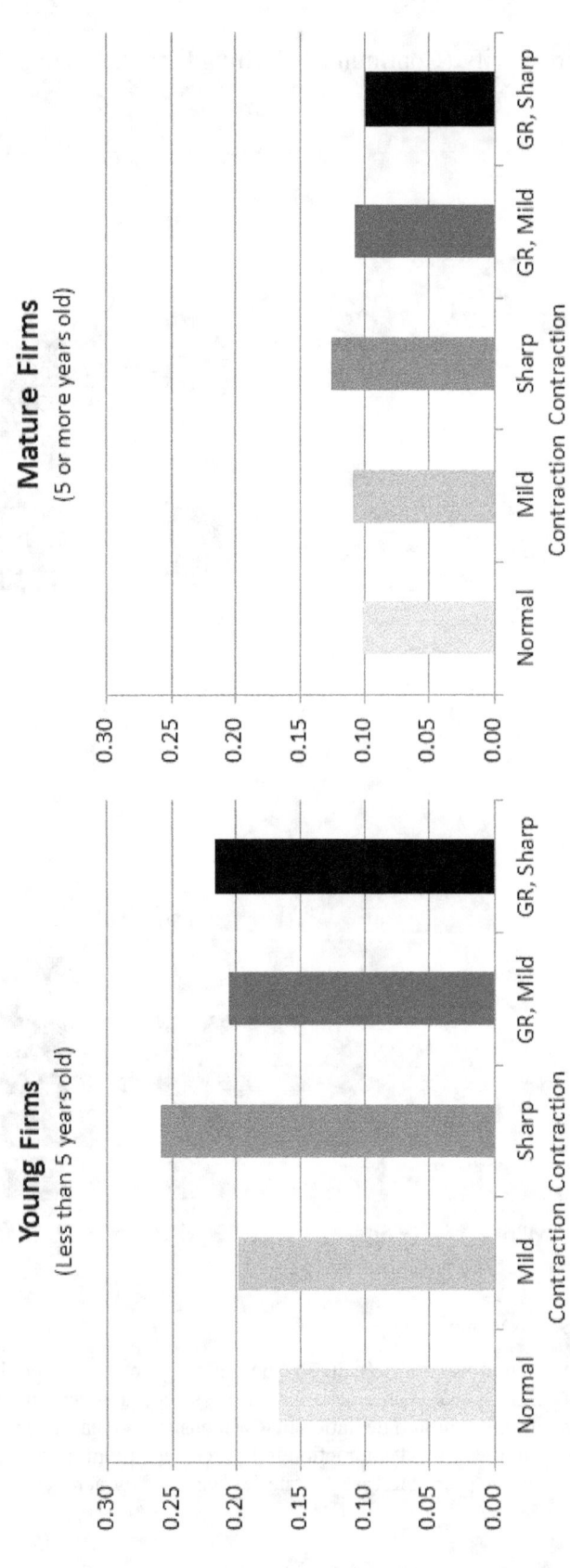

Source: Authors' calculations on the ASM, CM and LBD.

Notes: Depicted is the predicted difference in growth rates (high minus low) between an establishment one standard deviation above industry-by-year mean productivity and an establishment one standard deviation below industry-by-year mean productivity. Normal is zero change in state-level unemployment, mild contraction is 1 percentage point increase in state level unemployment, sharp contraction is 3 percentage point increase in state-level unemployment, GR is for period 2007-09.

Figure 6. Predicted Contribution of Reallocation to Aggregate (Industry-Level) Productivity

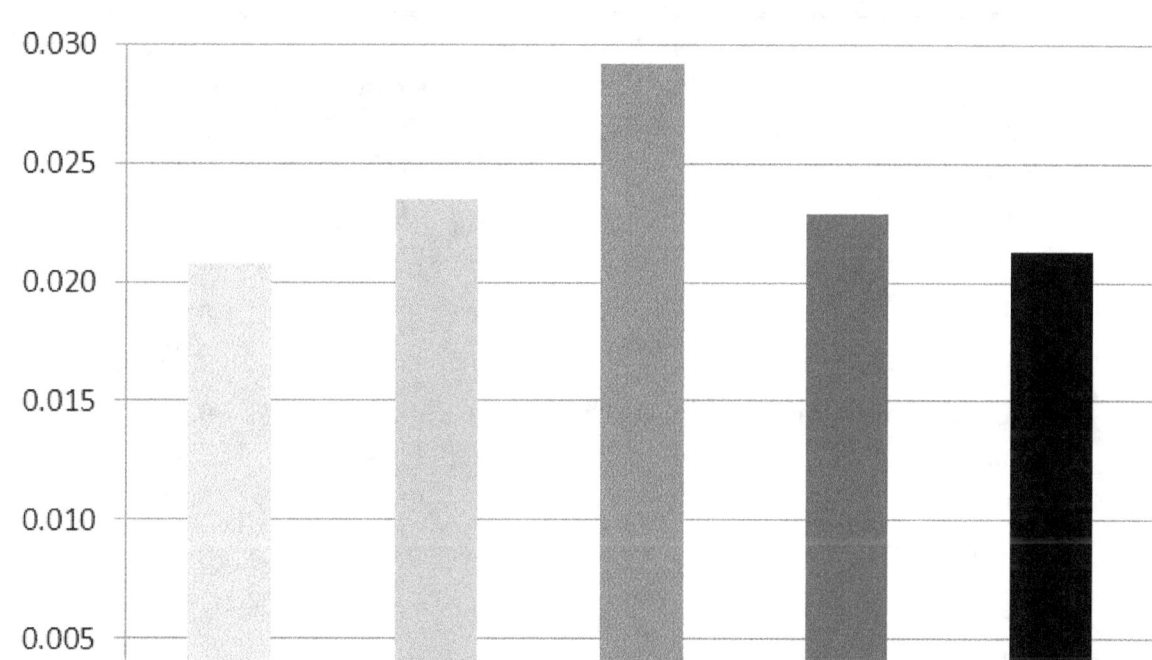

Source: Authors' calculations from estimated models.

Table 1. Descriptive Statistics, ASM/CM/LBD Matched Sample

	Mean	Standard Deviation
Overall Growth Rate (Continuers + Exit)	-0.17	0.65
Young	-0.26	0.85
Mature	-0.15	0.59
Establishment Exit	0.08	0.27
Young	0.15	0.35
Mature	0.07	0.25
Conditional Growth Rate (Continuers Only)	-0.01	0.38
Young	0.04	0.49
Mature	-0.02	0.35
Establishment Entry	0.07	0.25
TFP	0.000	0.360
Young	-0.011	0.353
Mature	0.003	0.362
Cycle	0.0004	0.0107
Young	0.19	0.39
GR	0.09	0.28
Years	1981-2010	
N (millions)	2.2	

Source: Authors' calculations on the ASM, CM and LBD.

Notes:
1. Statistics use propensity score weights to make the sample representative of the LBD. Statistics are not activity weighted.
2. Employment growth and exit are measured from period t to period $t+1$. Rates are in fractions (not percents).
3. TFP is the deviation of establishment-level log TFP from its' industry-year mean in year t so the mean is, by construction, equal to zero.
4. Cycle is the state-year change in the unemployment rate from t to $t+1$. Rates are in fractions (not percents).
5. Young is a dummy variable equal to one for establishments that belong to firms less than 5 years old.
6. GR is a dummy variable equal to one for years from 2007 to 2009.

Table 2. Share of Change in Net Employment Growth Due to Change in Job Creation in Periods of Net Contraction

	National		State
Period	**BDS (Annual)**	**BED (Quarterly)**	**BDS (Annual)**
Pre-Great Recession	0.21	0.28	0.39
Post-2007	0.61	0.59	0.65

Source: Authors' calculations on the BDS and BED.

Notes:

1. The calculations take advantage of the identity that Net = Job Creation – Job Destruction. For periods of net contraction lasting one or more periods, the cumulative change in net employment growth and cumulative change in job creation are calculated over the entire consecutive period of net contraction. In turn, these cumulative changes are cumulated further within the periods in the table. The share is the fraction of the overall cumulative change in net employment growth over the specified period accounted for by the overall change in job creation over the specified period.
2. For BDS, Pre-Great Recession is 1981-2007, Post-2007 is 2008-2011. For the BED, Pre-Great Recession is 1990:2-2007:3, Post-2007 is 2007:4-2012:1. As noted, these statistics are only calculated for periods with net employment growth less than zero. For example, this is 2007:4-2010:1 for the BED.
3. For the BDS National annual there are only 6 years of net contraction with only 2 years in the post 2007 period. For the BED quarterly, there are 22 quarters of net contraction with 9 quarters in the post-2008 period. For the BDS State Annual there are 393 state-year observations with net contraction with 112 state-year observations with net contractions in the post-2007 period.

Table 3. Job Flows and Change in the Unemployment Rate at the State-Level (Annual), 1981-2011

	Job Creation Rate	Job Destruction Rate	Reallocation Rate
Cycle	-0.631***	1.194***	0.563***
	(0.046)	(0.053)	(0.068)
GR*Cycle	-0.371***	-0.421***	-0.793***
	(0.079)	(0.079)	(0.128)
Trend	-0.168***	-0.136***	-0.304***
	(0.010)	(0.011)	(0.020)
N	1,581	1,581	1,581

* $p < 0.10$, ** $p < 0.05$, *** $p < 0.01$

Source: Authors' calculations on the BDS.

Notes:
1. GR is a dummy variable equal to one for years from 2008 to 2010 (job flows from March 2007 to March 2010).
2. Cycle is the *state*-year change in the unemployment rate.
3. All specifications include state fixed effects.
4. Standard errors in parentheses are clustered at the state level.

Table 4. Reallocation and Productivity over the Business Cycle

	Overall Growth Rate (Continuers + Exiters)		Exit		Conditional Growth Rate (Continuers Only)	
	(1)	(2)	(3)	(4)	(5)	(6)
TFP	0.157***	0.159***	-0.060***	-0.060***	0.041***	0.042***
	(0.006)	(0.006)	(0.003)	(0.003)	(0.003)	(0.003)
Cycle	-3.307***	-2.961***	0.671***	0.497***	-2.143***	-2.128***
	(0.459)	(0.483)	(0.176)	(0.179)	(0.247)	(0.286)
TFP*Cycle	1.542**	2.182**	-0.655***	-0.927***	0.494	0.534
	(0.643)	(0.862)	(0.226)	(0.265)	(0.412)	(0.567)
GR*TFP		0.030		-0.018*		-0.005
		(0.023)		(0.011)		(0.011)
GR*Cycle		-3.116**		1.581***		-0.126
		(1.349)		(0.523)		(0.770)
GR*TFP*Cycle		-2.961*		1.466**		0.066
		(1.619)		(0.684)		(0.764)
Year FE	yes	yes	yes	yes	yes	yes
State FE	yes	yes	yes	yes	yes	yes
Firm Size Class FE	yes	yes	yes	yes	yes	yes
N (millions)	2.2	2.2	2.2	2.2	2.1	2.1

* $p < 0.10$, ** $p < 0.05$, *** $p < 0.01$

Source: Authors' calculations on the ASM, CM and LBD.

Notes:
1. Regressions are weighted by propensity score weights. Weight calculation is described in the Appendix.
2. Standard errors (in parentheses) are clustered at the state level.
3. Employment growth and exit are measured from period t to period $t+1$. Regression for exit is a linear probability model where exit=1 if the establishment has positive activity in period t but no activity in period $t+1$.
4. TFP is the deviation of establishment-level log TFP from its' industry-year mean in year t.
5. GR is a dummy variable equal to one for years from 2007 to 2009 (reflecting outcomes from March 2007 to March 2010).
6. Cycle is the state-year change in the unemployment rate from t to $t+1$.

Table 5. Reallocation and Productivity over the Business Cycle By Firm Age

	Overall Growth Rate (Continuers + Exiters)		Exit		Conditional Growth Rate (Continuers Only)	
	(1)	(2)	(3)	(4)	(5)	(6)
Young	-0.059***	-0.054***	0.050***	0.049***	0.047***	0.050***
	(0.005)	(0.005)	(0.002)	(0.002)	(0.003)	(0.003)
TFP*Mature	0.138***	0.139***	-0.054***	-0.055***	0.034***	0.033***
	(0.007)	(0.007)	(0.003)	(0.003)	(0.003)	(0.003)
TFP*Young	0.237***	0.236***	-0.085***	-0.083***	0.075***	0.077***
	(0.013)	(0.015)	(0.006)	(0.006)	(0.006)	(0.007)
Cycle*Mature	-2.590***	-2.487***	0.345**	0.230	-2.047***	-2.183***
	(0.401)	(0.402)	(0.143)	(0.141)	(0.232)	(0.270)
Cycle*Young	-6.626***	-5.274***	2.196***	1.775***	-2.578***	-1.878***
	(0.988)	(1.152)	(0.407)	(0.463)	(0.412)	(0.455)
TFP*Cycle*Mature	0.674	1.112	-0.429*	-0.720***	-0.031	-0.193
	(0.620)	(0.733)	(0.234)	(0.235)	(0.354)	(0.538)
TFP*Cycle*Young	3.886**	4.336**	-1.147*	-1.088	2.476**	2.811**
	(1.568)	(2.016)	(0.649)	(0.759)	(1.030)	(1.110)
GR*TFP*Mature		0.015		-0.010		-0.005
		(0.029)		(0.014)		(0.007)
GR*TFP*Young		0.046		-0.030		-0.004
		(0.076)		(0.034)		(0.042)
GR*Cycle*Mature		-1.685		1.234**		0.769
		(1.268)		(0.505)		(0.758)
GR*Cycle*Young		-8.627***		2.940***		-4.152***
		(2.318)		(0.934)		(0.907)
GR*TFP*Cycle*Mature		-1.708		1.162		0.686
		(1.691)		(0.759)		(0.657)
GR*TFP*Cycle*Young		-3.566		0.965		-0.999
		(4.585)		(1.934)		(2.115)
Year FE	yes	yes	yes	yes	yes	yes
State FE	yes	yes	yes	yes	yes	yes
Firm Size Class FE	yes	yes	yes	yes	yes	yes
N (millions)	2.2	2.2	2.2	2.2	2.1	2.1

* $p < 0.10$, ** $p < 0.05$, *** $p < 0.01$
Source: Authors' calculations on the ASM, CM and LBD.

Notes: See notes to Table 4. Young (Mature) is establishments that belong to firms less than (greater than or equal to) 5 years old.

Table 6. Entry and Productivity over the Business Cycle

	Establishment Entry	
	(1)	(2)
TFP	-0.006***	-0.006***
	(0.002)	(0.002)
Cycle	-0.388***	-0.376***
	(0.136)	(0.142)
TFP*Cycle	0.274***	0.239**
	(0.075)	(0.103)
GR*TFP		0.006*
		(0.004)
GR*Cycle		-0.176
		(0.504)
GR*TFP*Cycle		-0.088
		(0.199)
Year FE	yes	yes
State FE	yes	yes
Firm Size Class FE	yes	yes
N (millions)	2.2	2.2

* $p < 0.10$, ** $p < 0.05$, *** $p < 0.01$

Source: Authors' calculations on the ASM, CM and LBD.

Notes:
1. Regressions are weighted by propensity score weights. Weight calculation is described in the Appendix.
2. Standard errors (in parentheses) are clustered at the state level.
3. Entry is measured from t-1 to t. Regression is linear probability model with entry=1 if this is first year of operation of establishment.
4. TFP is the deviation of establishment-level log TFP from its' industry-year mean in year t.
5. GR is a dummy variable equal to one for years from 2008 to 2010 (given t-1 to t).
6. Cycle is the state-year change in the unemployment rate from t-1 to t.

Appendix

A. Establishment-Level Data

A.1. Longitudinal Business Database

The Longitudinal Business Database (LBD) is a census of non-agricultural business establishments and firms with paid employees in the U.S. The LBD is comprised of survey and administrative records and is currently available from 1976-2011.[59] The LBD contains establishment-level information on payroll, employment, industry and geography.

We use the LBD to create our three outcome measures: overall growth (employment growth for continuers + exiters), establishment exit, and conditional growth (employment growth for continuers only). These outcome measures are created from t to $t+1$. For example, establishment exit = 1 if the establishment is active (has positive employment) in period t and is not active in period $t+1$.

We also use the LBD to create measures of establishment and firm age. Establishment age is calculated as the current year minus the first year the establishment appears in the LBD with positive employment. We calculate firm age as the age of the oldest establishment in the firm in the first year the firm appears in the LBD with positive employment. Establishments and firms are "young" if they are less than 5 years old and "mature" if they are 5 years old or older.

We also use the LBD to create a measure of firm size. We sum up the employment of all establishments in the firm to get firm size. The firm size class variable is created as shown below in Table A.1. We include this variable for firm size fixed effects in our regressions.

Table A.1. Firm Size Class Definition

Definition	Firm Size Class
Firm Employment < 250	1
250 ≤ Firm Employment < 500	2
500 ≤ Firm Employment < 1000	3
Firm Employment ≥ 1000	4

---

[59] The LBD and other establishment-level data used in this paper are available for use by qualified researchers with approved projects in secure Census Bureau Research Data Centers.

A.2. Census of Manufactures

The Census of Manufactures (CM) collects data from manufacturing establishments every 5 years in years ending in "2" and "7". All manufacturing establishments are sent forms except for very small establishments (less than five employees). Payroll and employment data for these very small establishments is available from administrative records. The Census Bureau uses the administrative data to impute other data items for these "administrative records cases." We drop administrative records cases from our dataset. We use CM data from 1972-2007.

The CM includes information on industry, geography, outputs and inputs. We use the CM in conjunction with the Annual Survey of Manufactures (described below) to calculate establishment-level TFP. Our TFP calculation methodology is described in Section B of this Appendix. We also use state and industry data from the CM.

A.3. Annual Survey of Manufactures

The Annual Survey of Manufactures (ASM) is collected in all non-CM years. The Census Bureau surveys roughly 50,000-70,000 manufacturing establishments in the ASM. We use ASM data from 1973-2010. The ASM is a series of 5-year panels, with new panels starting in years ending in "4" and "9". Probability of selection into the ASM sample is a function of industry and size.

Like the CM, the ASM also includes information on industry, geography, outputs, and inputs. We link data from the ASM and CM to calculate establishment-level TFP. Our TFP calculation methodology is described in Section B of this Appendix. We also use state and industry data from the ASM.

B. Measuring Establishment-Level Total Factor Productivity (TFP)

This section of the Appendix contains information on our calculation of establishment-level TFP. In calculating TFP, our primary data sources are the 1972-2010 ASM and CM data. We supplement these data with industry-level data from the Bureau of Economic Analysis (BEA), the Bureau of Labor Statistics (BLS), and the NBER-CES Manufacturing Industry Database.

B.1. Output

We calculate real establishment-level total output, Q_{et}, as shown in (B1).

$$\text{If the resulting } Q_{et} \text{ is positive, then } Q_{et} = \frac{(TVS_{et}+DF_{et}+DW_{et})}{PISHIP_{it}}$$

$$\text{else } Q_{et} = TVS_{et}/PISHIP_{it} \tag{B1}$$

where TVS_{et} is the total value of shipments for establishment e in year t, DF_{et} is the difference between the values of end-of-year and beginning-of-year finished goods inventories for establishment e in year t, DW_{et} is the difference between the values of end-of-year and beginning-of-year work-in-progress inventories for establishment e in year t, and $PISHIP_{it}$ is the industry-level shipments deflator.[60] Note, when components of DF or DW are missing, they are set to zero.

B.2. Labor

Labor, TH_{et}, is measured as total hours, calculated as shown in (B2).

$$\text{If } SW_{et} > 0 \text{ and } WW_{et} > 0 \text{ then } TH_{et} = (PH_{et} * SW_{et})/WW_{et}$$

$$\text{else } TH_{et} = PH_{et} \tag{B2}$$

where SW_{et} is the total annual payroll for establishment e in year t, WW_{et} is the payroll of production workers for establishment e in year t and PH_{et} is the number of hours worked by production workers for establishment e in year t.

B.3. Capital

We use the perpetual inventory method to calculate capital stocks where possible – separately for structures and equipment. Specifically:

$$K_{e,t+1} = (1 - \delta_{i,t+1})K_{et} + I_{e,t+1} \tag{B3}$$

where I denotes investment, and δ denotes the depreciation rate (at the industry level i). To use the perpetual inventory method, we must initialize capital stocks and have uninterrupted

---

[60] Industry-level deflators are at the 4-digit SIC industry level prior to 1997 and at the 6-digit NAICS industry level thereafter. The *PISHIP*, *PIMAT* and *PIEN* deflator are from the NBER-CES Manufacturing Industry Database.

investment data. Given the panel nature of the ASM and the varying availability of capital stock data, we apply the perpetual inventory method backwards through time in some cases.

We initialize capital stocks in the earliest possible year using book values adjusted for the ratio of real to book value of capital at roughly the 2-digit SIC or 3-digit NAICS level. The ratio of real to book value of capital is derived from BEA data.[61] We deflate capital expenditures using investment price deflators from the BLS at the 2-digit SIC or 3-digit NAICS level.

When we cannot initialize capital stocks using the method described above, we use a methodology similar to Bloom et al. (2013), imputing initial capital stocks for a relatively small number of additional cases (less than half a percent) using I/K ratios. Specifically, if the establishment was in the prior CM, we impute the initial capital stock for the establishment using the ratio of investment to the book value of capital stock (I/K ratio) in the prior CM. If the establishment was not in the prior CM, we use the industry-level I/K ratio, calculating a separate ratio for young (less than 5 years old) establishments.[62]

B.4. Materials

Real establishment-level non-energy materials costs, M_{et}, are calculated as shown in (B4).

$$M_{et} = (CP_{et} + CR_{et} + CW_{et})/PIMAT_{it} \tag{B4}$$

where CP_{et} is the cost of materials and parts for establishment e in year t, CR_{et} is the cost of resales (products bought and sold without further processing) for establishment e in year t, CW_{et} is the cost of work done for the establishment by others on the establishment's materials for establishment e in year t and $PIMAT_{it}$ is the industry-level materials deflator.

---

[61] SIC codes are used prior to 1997, and NAICS codes are used for 1997 and later. BEA provides only SIC/NAICS industry descriptions. These descriptions are converted into SIC codes (roughly SIC2, but some SIC3 groups) or NAICS codes (roughly NAICS3, but some NAICS3 and NAICS4 groups) using a concordance provided in "Local Area Personal Income and Employment Methodology" (April 2010) [www.bea.gov/regional/pdf/lapi2008/lapi2008.pdf].

[62] We use a hybrid approach for a small number of cases. We sought to avoid abrupt jumps in the capital stock at the establishment level when the needed imputation is for one year gaps in the data. Such gaps occur from the ASM panel rotation (e.g., establishment is in CM but not current ASM – then selected for subsequent ASM). In this method, we consider two alternative capital stock measures. One is using the I/K ratio imputation as noted in the text. The other is to use perpetual inventory to calculate the capital stock for the establishment filling in gap years in the establishment's data assuming the establishment had zero investment in the gap year. If this latter "gap" capital stock number is larger than the capital stock calculated using our version of the Bloom et al. (2013) method, we use it.

We calculate real establishment-level energy costs as shown in (B5).

$$E_{et} = (EE_{et} + CF_{et})/PIEN_{it} \tag{B5}$$

where EE_{et} is the cost of purchased electricity for establishment e in year t, CF_{et} is the cost of purchased fuels consumed for heat, power or the generation of electricity and $PIEN_{it}$ is the industry-level energy deflator.

B.5. Industry-Level Cost Shares

We calculate industry-level cost shares for each input using publicly available data from the BLS and the NBER-CES Manufacturing Industry Database. Our calculated cost shares are at the 4-digit SIC level prior to 1997 and at the 6-digit NAICS level thereafter.

We obtain the following industry-level cost measures from the NBER-CES data: capital expenditures on equipment (*EQUIP*); capital expenditures on structures (*PLANT*); materials and energy costs (*MATCOST*); energy costs (*ENERGY*) and labor costs (*PAY*).[63] We obtain industry-level data from the BLS on capital income (*EQKY* and *STKY*), productive capital stock (*EQPK* and *STPK*), and capital composition (*EQKC* and *STKC*). These can be used to back out rental prices for capital and equipment.

Total cost for industry i in year t is calculated as shown in (B6).

$$TC_{it} = (EQRKL_{it} * EQUIP_{it}) + (STRKL_{it} * PLANT_{it}) + PAY_{it} + MATCOST_{it} \tag{B6}$$

where *EQRKL* and *STRKL* are rental prices we calculate as shown in (B7).[64]

$$EQRKL_{it} = \frac{EQKY_{it}}{EQPK_{it}*EQKC_{it}} \qquad STRKL_{it} = \frac{STKY_{it}}{STPK_{it}*STKC_{it}} \tag{B7}$$

Since industry cost shares can be noisy and using current year cost shares presumes that factor adjustment costs are entirely absent (see Syverson (2011) for more discussion), we use the time averaged cost share between t and t-1 in our TFP calculation. The first year of an industry coding change (1987 and 1997) and the first year of our data (1972) are exceptions. For these years, we use the cost share in year t. We have also considered cost shares that are the time

---

[63] The NBER-CES Manufacturing Industry Database is currently only available through 2009. We imputed 2010 values using related variables in the 2010 ASM microdata and data available from the BEA and the BLS.
[64] We note the BLS releases rental prices for equipment and structures capital as indices. Our rental prices converted to indices match the BLS rental prices exactly.

averages over all periods (separately for the NAICS and SIC years). We find TFP so calculated has a correlation very close to 1 (0.995) with the TFP we use in our analysis.

B.6.   Calculation of TFP

We calculate establishment-level log TFP as shown in (B8). We only calculate TFP for establishments with positive values for each of the establishment-level inputs and output.

$$LTFP_{et} = \log(Q_{et}) - IAKE_{it} * \log(KSTEQ_{et}) - IAKS_{it} * \log(KSTST_{et})$$

$$-IAL_{it} * \log(TH_{et}) - IAM_{it} * \log(M_{et}) - IAE_{it} * \log(E_{et}) \quad (B8)$$

For the final sample used in the analysis, note we exclude observations that appear to have been imputed using the industry average ratios of shipments and materials to payroll. Our exclusion criteria use the methods developed and used by Dunne (1998) and Roberts and Supina (1996). The industry average ratio of imputing is arguably the most problematic item imputation approach used by the Census Bureau in terms of distorting the relationships in the micro data. We exclude about 7,000 establishments using this method. Note we detect more problematic Dunne/Roberts/Supina cases in Census years and in the post-2000 period. Both make sense as Census years there are many more small establishments surveyed compared to an ASM year and it appears as well that item imputation rates rose in the post-2000 period. Like Baily, Hulten and Campbell (1992) we also trim those observations that deviate from the industry/year mean of TFP by more than 200 log points in absolute value. This trims less than 1 percent of the upper and lower tails of the within industry-year TFP distribution.

C. Creation of Propensity Score Weights

Although the primary dependent variable for this analysis, TFP, is only available for observations in the ASM/CM, the LBD contains accurate establishment-level data on employment, size, payroll, industry classification, job creation and job destruction for the entire universe of manufacturing establishments in the United States. Thus, we match ASM/CM establishments to the LBD and use LBD measures of the above variables in our regression analyses. We refer to the integrated data as the ASM/CM/LBD sample. Furthermore, to ensure the ASM/CM/LBD sample is representative of the entire universe of manufacturing establishments, we calculate propensity scores to generate an appropriate set of population weights.

We match establishments in the ASM/CM to LBD establishments by year and "LBD Number". LBD Number is an establishment identifier that exists on both datasets.[65] For each establishment in the LBD for each year from 1981 to 2010, we create a dummy variable that is equal to one if the establishment is in both the ASM/CM and the LBD for that year and equal to zero if the establishment is only the LBD ("ASM/CM Dummy"). The ASM/CM Dummy for each year then serves as the dependent variable in the regressions that create the propensity scores. Note in CM years, establishments that are administrative records cases have all imputed data, and we set the ASM/CM dummy=0 for such cases.

The propensity scores are created from a logistic regression where the ASM/CM Dummy is the dependent variable and a series of dummy variables that capture establishment characteristics are the independent variables. The variables in the logistic regression analysis are: a dummy for whether an establishment is part of a multi-unit entity, establishment size class (measured by employment), payroll and detailed industry codes. These variables are obvious candidates for this analysis since the probability of selection into the ASM sample and the selection of administrative records cases in the CM vary explicitly by industry and size. We also note ASM sampling and administrative records case thresholds vary across years so it is critical to estimate the propensity score models separately by year. This is especially critical given our approach of combining CM and ASM years in a common sample.

From the LBD (and related sources), we have 4-digit SIC codes through 1996 and 6-digit NAICS codes for 1997 forward. We discovered use of dummy variables corresponding directly to 4-digit SIC codes and 6-digit NAICS codes leads to convergence issues for our logistic regression in some years. This is not surprising given a small number of detailed industries have a relatively small number of observations in specific years. Although we could easily achieve convergence of our logistic model by using broad industry categories corresponding to 2-digit SIC codes and 3-digit NAICS codes, we use a hybrid method, described below, to preserve as much variation as possible at the detailed industry level.

---

[65] While linking the datasets by LBD Number is straightforward, there are a small percentage of establishment-year observations that do not match due to timing issues between the ASM/CM and the LBD.

We create modified detailed industry classifications for this analysis by implementing the following procedure. First, we count the number of establishments per 4-digit SIC (6-digit NAICS). Second, we identify the 4-digit SIC (6-digit NAICS) with the maximum number of observations in its 3-digit SIC (4-digit NAICS) universe. Next, we match every 4-digit SIC (6-digit NAICS) to the 4-digit SIC (6-digit NAICS) with the maximum number of establishment observations within the relevant 3-digit SIC (4-digit NAICS) family. If a 4-digit SIC (6-digit NAICS) is associated with 20 or fewer establishments in the full dataset, then its detailed industry is recoded with the 4-digit SIC (6-digit NAICS) corresponding to the maximum within the 3-digit SIC (4-digit NAICS) family.

To confirm our propensity score matching approach is reasonable we compare manufacturing employment in the LBD to the weighted employment calculated for the ASM/CM/LBD sample and the weighted employment for those establishments in the ASM/CM reporting values for TFP. Figure C.1 shows we match annual average total employment quite well with the weighted samples – and obviously are substantially short in the unweighted samples. The critical aspect of the weighting is to make the weighted sample match the size and age distributions of the full LBD. Figures C.2 and C.3 show that the weighted samples do exactly this – the unweighted samples have, as expected, higher shares of large and mature establishments. The weighted samples match the full LBD size and age distributions well.

Figure C.1. Annual Average Total Employment in Manufacturing

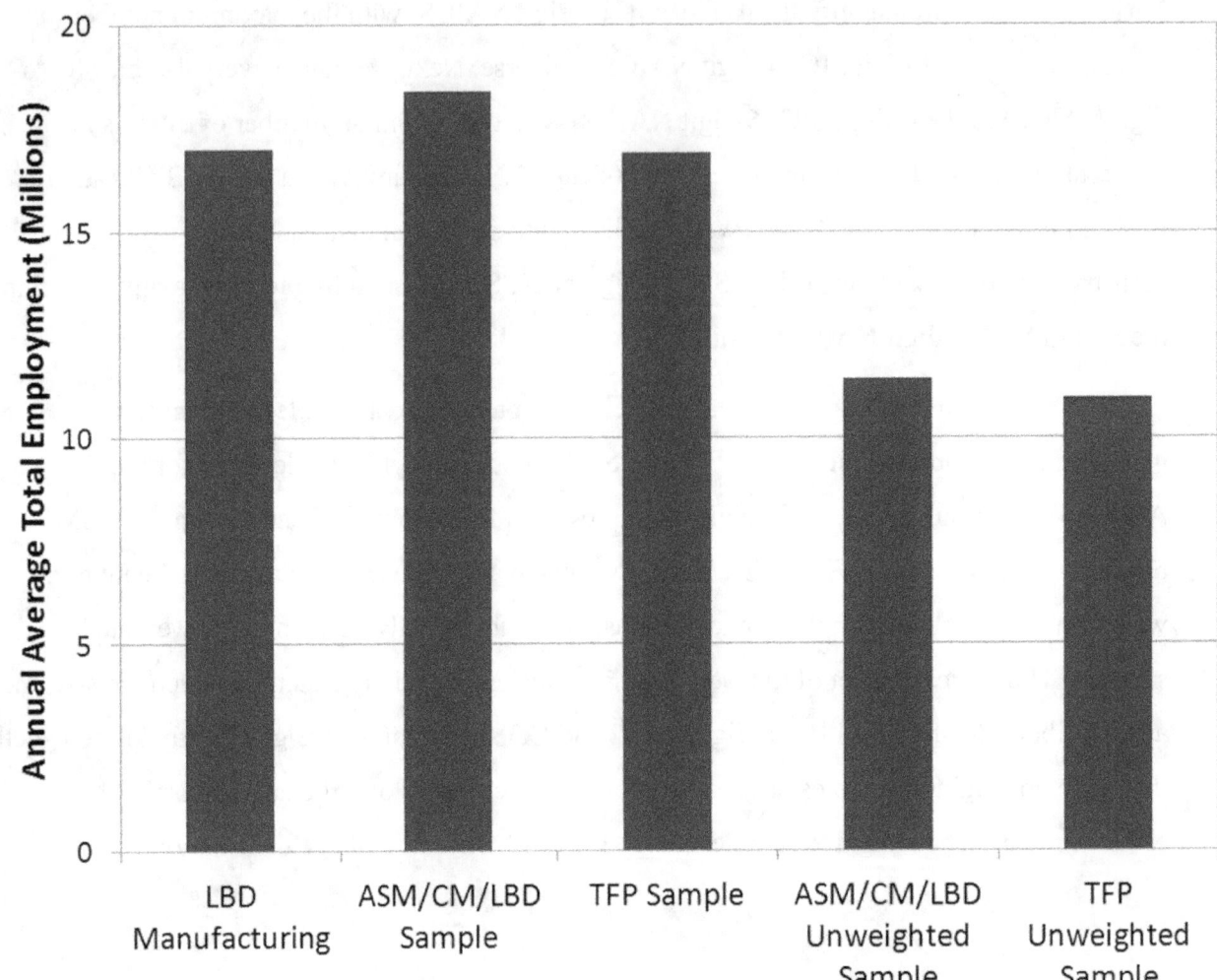

Source: Authors' calculations on the ASM, CM and LBD.

Notes:
1. LBD Manufacturing includes all manufacturing establishments in the LBD from 1981-2010.
2. ASM/CM/LBD Sample is all ASM/CM establishments that match to the LBD from 1981-2010. Statistics weighted by our created propensity score weight.
3. TFP Sample is all ASM/CM establishments that match to the LBD for which we can calculate TFP from 1981-2010. Statistics weighted by our created propensity score weight.
4. ASM/CM/LBD Unweighted Sample is the ASM/CM Sample where statistics are unweighted.
5. TFP Unweighted Sample is the TFP Sample where statistics are unweighted.

Figure C.2. Percent of Observations by Establishment Size Class

Source: Authors' calculations on the ASM, CM and LBD.

Notes:
1. LBD Manufacturing includes all manufacturing establishments in the LBD from 1981-2010.
2. ASM/CM/LBD Sample is all ASM/CM establishments that match to the LBD from 1981-2010. Statistics weighted by our created propensity score weight.
3. TFP Sample is all ASM/CM establishments that match to the LBD for which we can calculate TFP from 1981-2010. Statistics weighted by our created propensity score weight.
4. ASM/CM/LBD Unweighted Sample is the ASM/CM Sample where statistics are unweighted.
5. TFP Unweighted Sample is the TFP Sample where statistics are unweighted.

Figure C.3. Percent of Observations by Establishment Age

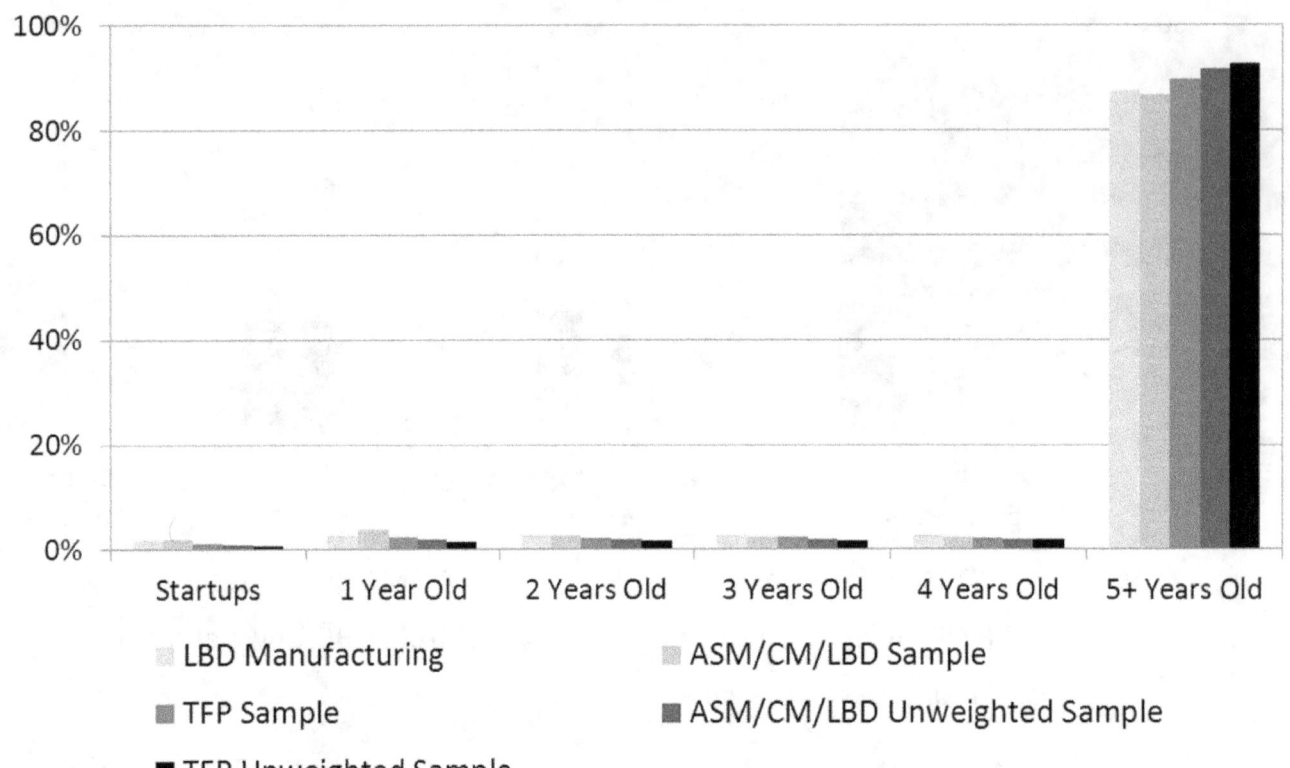

Source: Authors' calculations on the ASM, CM and LBD.

Notes:
1. LBD Manufacturing includes all manufacturing establishments in the LBD from 1981-2010.
2. ASM/CM/LBD Sample is all ASM/CM establishments that match to the LBD from 1981-2010. Statistics weighted by our created propensity score weight.
3. TFP Sample is all ASM/CM establishments that match to the LBD for which we can calculate TFP from 1981-2010. Statistics weighted by our created propensity score weight.
4. ASM/CM/LBD Unweighted Sample is the ASM/CM Sample where statistics are unweighted.
5. TFP Unweighted Sample is the TFP Sample where statistics are unweighted.

D. DHS Measures of Job Creation and Destruction

The job creation (*JC*) and job destruction (*JD*) rates for establishment *e* in group *q* in time *t* are defined in the following manner:[66]

$$JC_{qt} = \sum_{e \in Q+} (X_{eqt}/X_{qt}) \, g_{eqt} \tag{D.1}$$

$$JD_{qt} = \sum_{e \in Q-} (X_{eqt}/X_{qt}) \, |g_{eqt}| \tag{D.2}$$

where:

$$X_{eqt} = .5(E_{eqt} + E_{eq,t-1}) \tag{D.3}$$

$$g_{eqt} = \Delta E_{eqt}/X_{eqt} \tag{D.4}$$

Total job reallocation (*REALL*) is the sum of the job creation and job destruction rates (*REALL=JC+JD*) and the net employment growth rate (*NET*) is the job creation rate less the job destruction rate (*NET= JC-JD*).

---

[66] $Q+$ captures expanding establishments including startups and $Q-$ contracting establishments including shutdowns.

E. Sensitivity Analysis Figures and Tables

Figure E.1. Job Flows and the Business Cycle -- Trends

A. Annual, 1981-2011

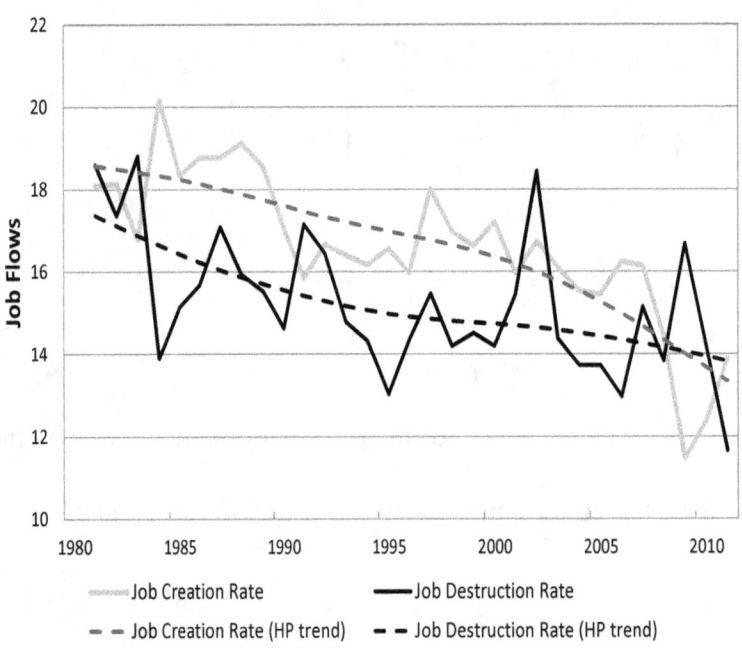

B. Quarterly, 1990:2-2012:1

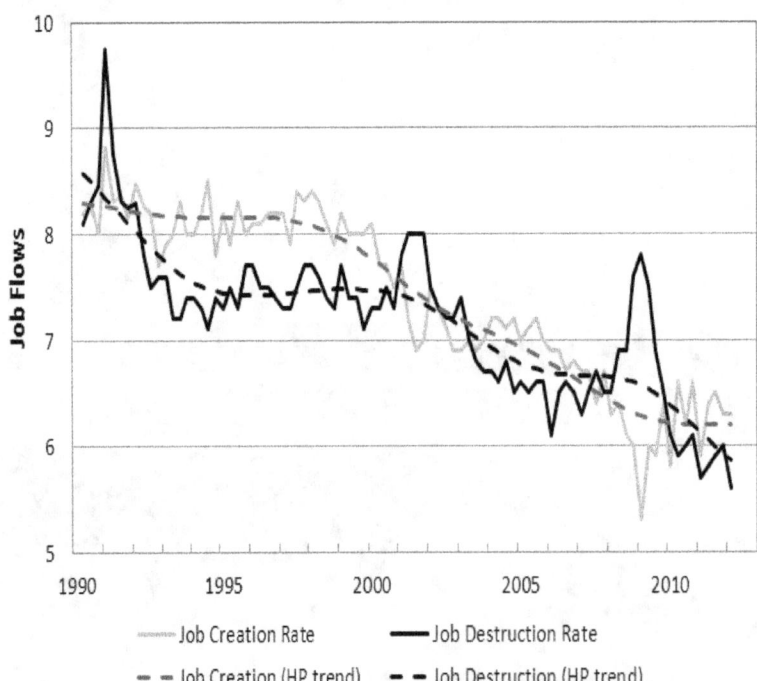

Source: Authors calculations using the BDS (Annual), BED (Quarterly) and CPS.

Note: Cycle is the change in the unemployment rate.

Figure E.2. Job Flows and the Business Cycle, *Manufacturing Sector*, 1981-2011

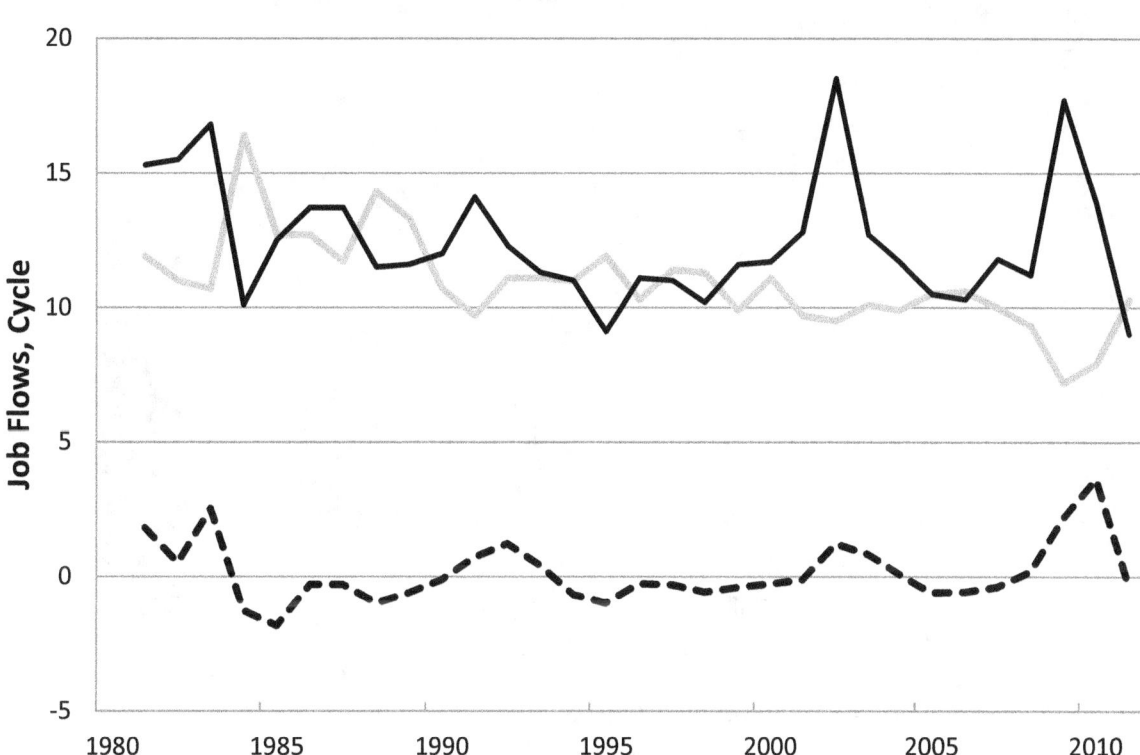

Source: Authors' calculations on the BDS.

Notes:
1. Cycle is the year change in the national unemployment rate. These have been timed appropriately with the BDS.
2. Job flows for year *t* reflect the changes from March in year *t*-1 to March in year *t*.

Figure E.3. Differences in Conditional Growth Rates (Continuing Establishments) Between High and Low Productivity Establishments Over the Business Cycle

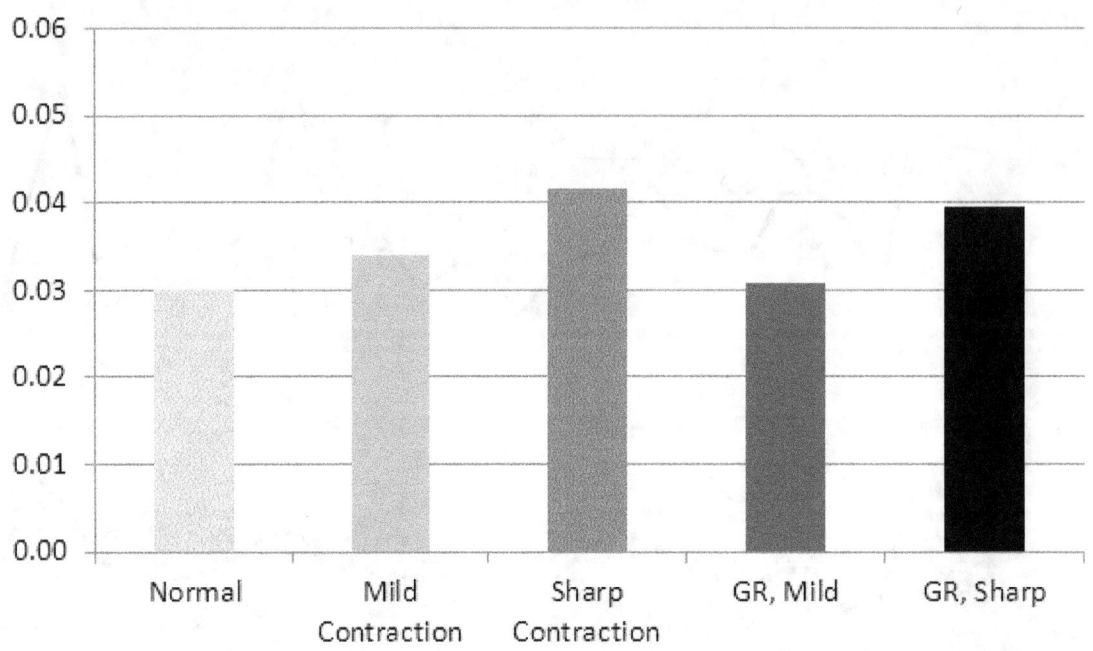

Source: Authors' calculations on the ASM, CM and LBD.

Notes: Depicted is the predicted difference in growth rates between an establishment one standard deviation above industry-by-year mean productivity and an establishment one standard deviation below industry-by-year mean productivity. Normal is zero change in state-level unemployment, mild contraction is 1 percentage point increase in state level unemployment, sharp contraction is 3 percentage point increase in state-level unemployment, GR is for period 2007-09.

Figure E.4. Difference in Exit Rates Between Low and High Productivity Establishments Over the Business Cycle: By Firm Age

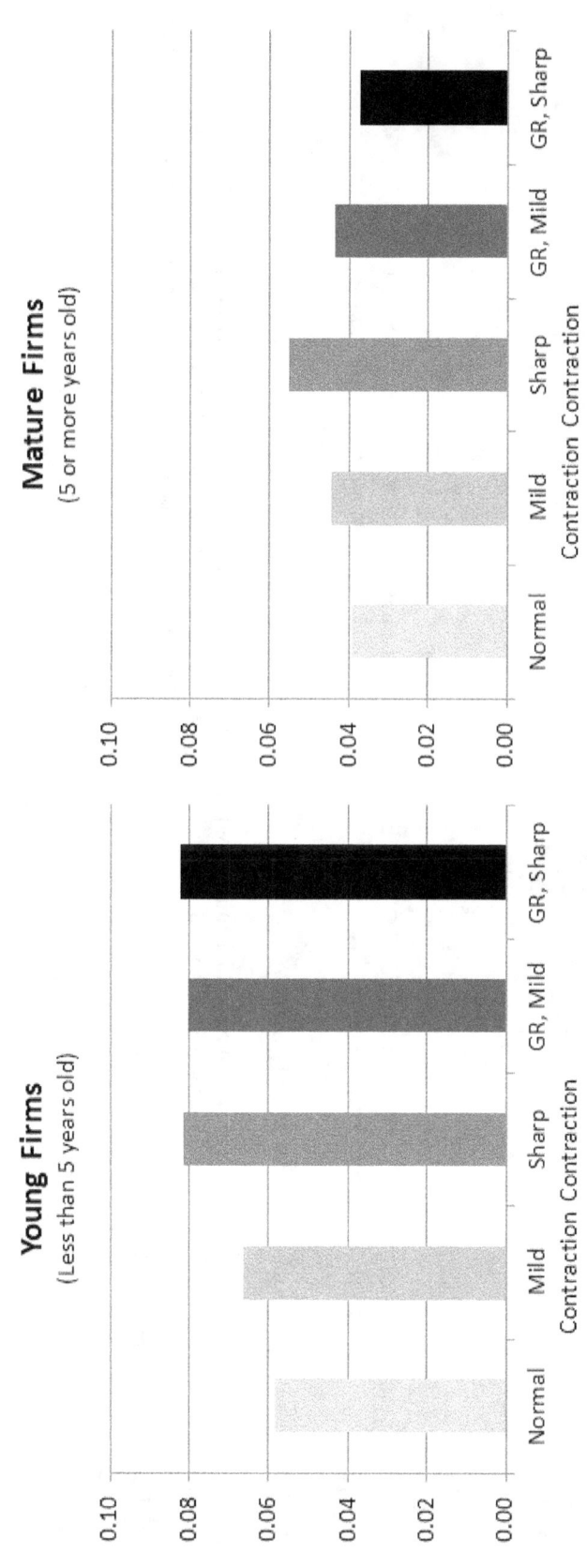

Source: Authors' calculations on the ASM, CM and LBD.

Notes: Depicted is the predicted difference in probability of exit (low minus high) between an establishment one standard deviation above industry-by-year mean productivity and an establishment one standard deviation below industry-by-year mean productivity. Normal is zero change in state-level unemployment, mild contraction is 1 percentage point increase in state level unemployment, sharp contraction is 3 percentage point increase in state-level unemployment, GR is for period 2007-09.

Figure E.5. Differences in Conditional Growth Rates (Continuing Establishments) Between High and Low Productivity Establishments Over the Business Cycle: By Firm Age

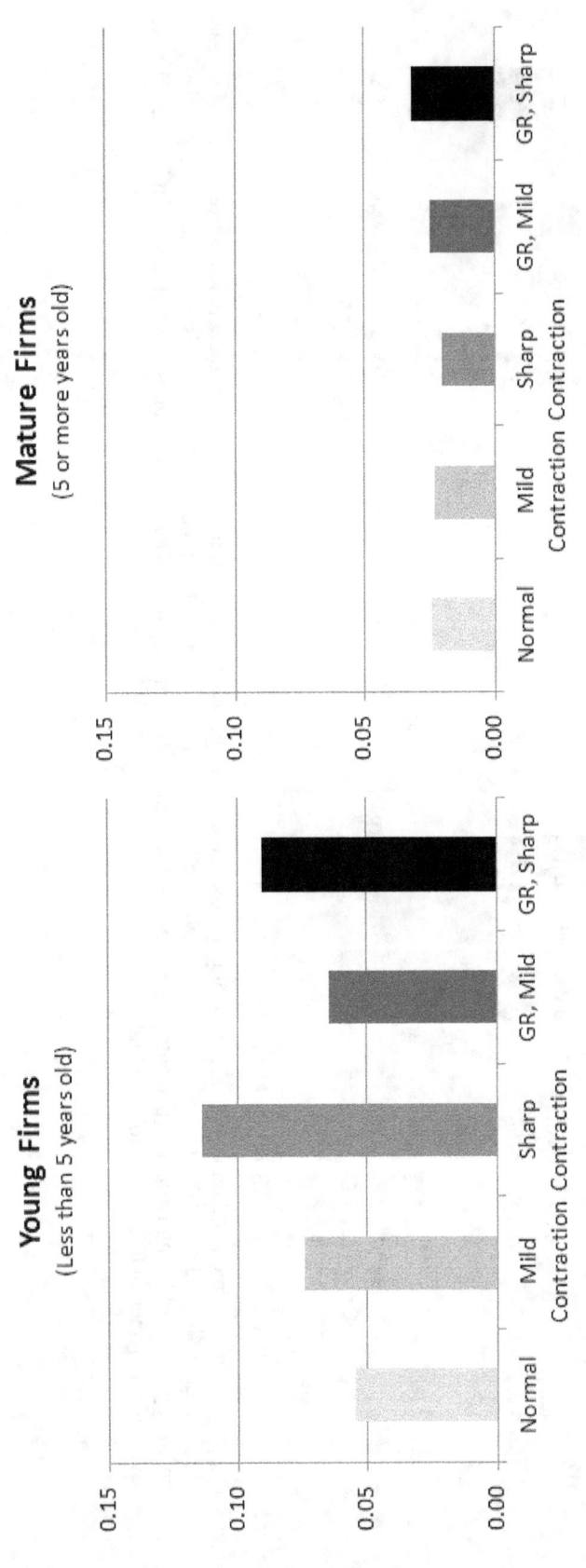

Source: Authors' calculations on the ASM, CM and LBD.

Notes: Depicted is the predicted difference in growth rates (high minus low) between an establishment one standard deviation above industry-by-year mean productivity and an establishment one standard deviation below industry-by-year mean productivity. Normal is zero change in state-level unemployment, mild contraction is 1 percentage point increase in state level unemployment, sharp contraction is 3 percentage point increase in state-level unemployment, GR is for period 2007-09.

Table E.1. Job Flows and Change in the *State-Level* Unemployment Rate (Annual) using both Great Recession and 1981-83 Recession Interactions

	Job Creation Rate	Job Destruction Rate	Reallocation Rate
Cycle	-0.551***	1.204***	0.652***
	(0.062)	(0.059)	(0.077)
80sR*Cycle	-0.234	-0.026	-0.261
	(0.124)	(0.144)	(0.219)
GR*Cycle	-0.440***	-0.429***	-0.869***
	(0.073)	(0.083)	(0.109)
Trend	-0.173***	-0.137***	-0.309***
	(0.011)	(0.011)	(0.021)
N	1,581	1,581	1,581

* $p < 0.10$, ** $p < 0.05$, *** $p < 0.01$

Source: Authors' calculations on the BDS.

Notes:
1. 80sR is a dummy variable equal to one for years from 1981 to 1983 (job flows from March 1980 to March 1983). GR is a dummy variable equal to one for years from 2008 to 2010 (job flows from March 2007 to March 2010).
2. Cycle is the *state*-year change in the unemployment rate.
3. Standard errors in parentheses clustered at the state level.

Table E.2. Job Flows and Change in the *State-Level* Unemployment Rate (Annual), *Age of Establishment*

	Job Creation Rates		Job Destruction Rates	
	Young	Mature	Young	Mature
Cycle	-1.402***	-0.266***	1.253***	0.669***
	(0.128)	(0.033)	(0.079)	(0.046)
GR*Cycle	-0.609***	-0.015	0.162	-0.083
	(0.170)	(0.052)	(0.118)	(0.062)
Trend	-0.083***	-0.094***	-0.077***	-0.115***
	(0.011)	(0.006)	(0.012)	(0.009)
N	1,581	1,581	1,581	1,581

* $p < 0.10$, ** $p < 0.05$, *** $p < 0.01$

Source: Authors' calculations on the BDS.

Notes:
1. GR is a dummy variable equal to one for years from 2008 to 2010 (job flows from March 2007 to March 2010).
2. Cycle is the *state*-year change in the unemployment rate.
3. All specifications include state fixed effects.
4. Standard errors in parentheses are clustered at the state level.

Table E.3. Reallocation and Productivity Over the Business Cycle, *No Year Effects*

	Overall Growth Rate (Continuers + Exiters)		Exit		Conditional Growth Rate (Continuers Only)	
	(1)	(2)	(3)	(4)	(5)	(6)
GR		-0.097***		0.027***		-0.044***
		(0.011)		(0.005)		(0.006)
TFP	0.157***	0.158***	-0.060***	-0.060***	0.041***	0.042***
	(0.006)	(0.006)	(0.003)	(0.003)	(0.003)	(0.003)
Cycle	-4.333***	-3.652***	0.876***	0.644***	-2.813***	-2.564***
	(0.330)	(0.376)	(0.137)	(0.147)	(0.141)	(0.174)
TFP*Cycle	1.550**	2.216**	-0.658***	-0.924***	0.500	0.595
	(0.667)	(0.879)	(0.229)	(0.269)	(0.428)	(0.578)
GR*TFP		0.029		-0.017*		-0.004
		(0.022)		(0.011)		(0.010)
GR*Cycle		1.047**		-0.145		0.719**
		(0.467)		(0.235)		(0.332)
GR*TFP*Cycle		-3.148*		1.464**		-0.157
		(1.620)		(0.688)		(0.749)
Year FE	no	no	no	no	no	no
State FE	yes	yes	yes	yes	yes	yes
Firm Size Class FE	yes	yes	yes	yes	yes	yes
N (millions)	2.2	2.2	2.2	2.2	2.1	2.1

* $p < 0.10$, ** $p < 0.05$, *** $p < 0.01$

Source: Authors' calculations on the ASM, CM and LBD.

Notes:
1. Regressions are weighted by propensity score weights. Weight calculation is described in the data appendix.
2. Standard errors (in parentheses) are clustered at the state level.
3. Employment growth and exit are measured from period t to period $t+1$. Regression for exit is a linear probability model where exit=1 if the establishment has positive activity in period t but no activity in period $t+1$.
4. TFP is the deviation of establishment-level log TFP from its' industry-year mean in year t.
5. GR is a dummy variable equal to one for years from 2007 to 2009.
6. Cycle is the state-year change in the unemployment rate from t to $t+1$.

Table E.4. Reallocation and Productivity over the Business Cycle, *No State Effects*

	Overall Growth Rate (Continuers + Exiters)		Exit		Conditional Growth Rate (Continuers Only)	
	(1)	(2)	(3)	(4)	(5)	(6)
TFP	0.155***	0.157***	-0.059***	-0.060***	0.041***	0.041***
	(0.006)	(0.006)	(0.002)	(0.002)	(0.003)	(0.003)
Cycle	-3.797***	-3.272***	0.891***	0.622***	-2.195***	-2.189***
	(0.561)	(0.542)	(0.233)	(0.203)	(0.247)	(0.289)
TFP*Cycle	1.552**	2.184**	-0.658***	-0.926***	0.500	0.541
	(0.646)	(0.869)	(0.227)	(0.267)	(0.413)	(0.568)
GR*TFP		0.031		-0.019*		-0.005
		(0.022)		(0.011)		(0.011)
GR*Cycle		-4.639***		2.383***		-0.044
		(1.735)		(0.656)		(0.787)
GR*TFP*Cycle		-2.985*		1.472**		0.060
		(1.625)		(0.685)		(0.768)
Year FE	yes	yes	yes	yes	yes	yes
State FE	no	no	no	no	no	no
Firm Size Class FE	yes	yes	yes	yes	yes	yes
N (millions)	2.2	2.2	2.2	2.2	2.1	2.1

* $p < 0.10$, ** $p < 0.05$, *** $p < 0.01$

Source: Authors' calculations on the ASM, CM and LBD.

Notes:
1. Regressions are weighted by propensity score weights. Weight calculation is described in the Appendix.
2. Standard errors (in parentheses) are clustered at the state level.
3. Employment growth and exit are measured from period t to period $t+1$. Regression for exit is a linear probability model where exit=1 if the establishment has positive activity in period t but no activity in period $t+1$.
4. TFP is the deviation of establishment-level log TFP from its' industry-year mean in year t.
5. GR is a dummy variable equal to one for years from 2007 to 2009 (reflecting outcomes from March 2007 to March 2010).
6. Cycle is the state-year change in the unemployment rate from t to $t+1$.

Table E.5. Reallocation and Productivity over the Business Cycle,
Cycle is Change in Employment-to-Population Ratio

	Overall Growth Rate (Continuers + Exiters)		Exit		Conditional Growth Rate (Continuers Only)	
	(1)	(2)	(3)	(4)	(5)	(6)
TFP	0.158***	0.159***	-0.060***	-0.061***	0.042***	0.041***
	(0.006)	(0.006)	(0.003)	(0.003)	(0.003)	(0.003)
Cycle	2.624***	2.451***	-0.666***	-0.561***	1.393***	1.424***
	(0.438)	(0.457)	(0.151)	(0.162)	(0.223)	(0.264)
TFP*Cycle	-1.357**	-1.936**	0.660**	0.963***	-0.270	-0.162
	(0.692)	(0.774)	(0.300)	(0.278)	(0.386)	(0.516)
GR*TFP		0.032		-0.020*		-0.007
		(0.023)		(0.011)		(0.011)
GR*Cycle		1.422		-0.878**		-0.267
		(0.882)		(0.378)		(0.753)
GR*TFP*Cycle		3.229*		-1.849**		-0.650
		(1.893)		(0.908)		(0.810)
Year FE	yes	yes	yes	yes	yes	yes
State FE	yes	yes	yes	yes	yes	yes
Firm Size Class FE	yes	yes	yes	yes	yes	yes
N (millions)	2.2	2.2	2.2	2.2	2.1	2.1

* $p < 0.10$, ** $p < 0.05$, *** $p < 0.01$

Source: Authors' calculations on the ASM, CM and LBD.

Notes:
1. Regressions are weighted by propensity score weights. Weight calculation is described in the Appendix.
2. Standard errors (in parentheses) are clustered at the state level.
3. Employment growth and exit are measured from period t to period $t+1$. Regression for exit is a linear probability model where exit=1 if the establishment has positive activity in period t but no activity in period $t+1$.
4. TFP is the deviation of establishment-level log TFP from its' industry-year mean in year t.
5. GR is a dummy variable equal to one for years from 2007 to 2009 (reflecting outcomes from March 2007 to March 2010).
6. Cycle is the state-year change in the employment-to-population ratio from t to $t+1$.

Table E.6. Reallocation and Productivity over the Business Cycle, *Excluding 1981-83*

	Overall Growth Rate (Continuers + Exiters)		Exit		Conditional Growth Rate (Continuers Only)	
	(1)	(2)	(3)	(4)	(5)	(6)
TFP	0.156***	0.157***	-0.060***	-0.061***	0.039***	0.039***
	(0.007)	(0.007)	(0.003)	(0.003)	(0.003)	(0.003)
Cycle	-3.350***	-2.918***	0.695***	0.465**	-2.153***	-2.158***
	(0.505)	(0.537)	(0.205)	(0.200)	(0.249)	(0.304)
TFP*Cycle	0.988*	1.474**	-0.470**	-0.751**	0.281	0.092
	(0.551)	(0.717)	(0.230)	(0.291)	(0.346)	(0.524)
GR*TFP		0.031		-0.018		-0.002
		(0.023)		(0.011)		(0.011)
GR*Cycle		-2.997**		1.597***		0.031
		(1.437)		(0.528)		(0.811)
GR*TFP*Cycle		-2.245		1.288*		0.516
		(1.556)		(0.715)		(0.746)
Year FE	yes	yes	yes	yes	yes	yes
State FE	yes	yes	yes	yes	yes	yes
Firm Size Class FE	yes	yes	yes	yes	yes	yes
N (millions)	1.9	1.9	1.9	1.9	1.8	1.8

* $p < 0.10$, ** $p < 0.05$, *** $p < 0.01$

Source: Authors' calculations on the ASM, CM and LBD.

Notes:
1. Regressions are weighted by propensity score weights. Weight calculation is described in the Appendix.
2. Standard errors (in parentheses) are clustered at the state level.
3. Employment growth and exit are measured from period t to period $t+1$. Regression for exit is a linear probability model where exit=1 if the establishment has positive activity in period t but no activity in period $t+1$.
4. TFP is the deviation of establishment-level log TFP from its' industry-year mean in year t.
5. GR is a dummy variable equal to one for years from 2007 to 2009 (reflecting outcomes from March 2007 to March 2010).
6. Cycle is the state-year change in the unemployment rate from t to $t+1$.